Client Development
for SOLO & SMALL FIRM LAWYERS

From LawyerAvenue Press
Career Resources for a Life in the Law

Client Development for Solo & Small Firm Lawyers
Insight, Advice, Tactics & Strategies
By Robert Lesser • $30 / 202 pages

The Hidden Legal Job Market
Law Jobs Aren't Always Where You Think They Are
By Richard L. Hermann • $30 / 254 pages

The New What Can You Do With a Law Degree?
A Lawyer's Guide to Career Satisfaction Inside, Outside & Around the Law
By Larry Richard & Tanya Hanson • $30 / 220 pages

Solo by Choice, Second Edition
How to Be the Lawyer You Always Wanted to Be
By Carolyn Elefant • $45 / 306 pages

Becoming a Rural Lawyer
A Personal Guide to Establishing a Small Town Practice
By Bruce M. Cameron • $30 / 148 pages

How to Litigate
The Crash Course for Trial Counsel
By Martin L. Grayson • $30 / 170 pages

Small Firms, Big Opportunity
How to Get Hired (and Succeed) in the New Legal Economy
By Linda Calvert Hanson, Samantha Williams • $30 / 168 pages

All titles are available at Amazon.com

Client Development
for SOLO & SMALL FIRM LAWYERS

INSIGHT, ADVICE, TACTICS & STRATEGIES

ROBERT LESSER

DecisionBooks
SEATTLE, WASHINGTON

Published by **LawyerAvenue Press** and its imprint DecisionBooks

Copyright © 2016 Robert Lesser. All rights reserved.

Printed in the United States of America. No part of this book may be reproduced, stored in a retrieval system, or transmitted in any form or by any means, electronic, mechanical, photocopying, recording, or otherwise, without the prior written permission of Avenue Productions, Inc.

Cover and interior design by Rose Michelle Taverniti

Volume discounts available from LawyerAvenue Press. Email to decisionbooks@gmail.com.

*This book is dedicated to my wife, Debbie,
and my sons, Eric and Jeffrey.
They are the reason for every worthwhile thing
I have ever undertaken or accomplished.*

Table of Contents

SECTION I: INTERVIEWING AND SIGNING UP CLIENTS

1. Lawyering is a service business 14
2. Choosing clients with care 17
3. The attorney-client privilege 19
4. The initial client interview 21
5. Judging the client and his story 24
6. Helping the client identify the real problem 26
7. Things the client has to be told 29
8. Don't over-promise as a way to sign a new client 33
9. When you don't like the client 35
10. For some clients, just say "no" 37

SECTION II: STRATEGIES FOR EXPANDING YOUR CLIENT BASE

1. Turning non-clients into clients 42
2. Keeping your name at the top of your client's mind 44
3. Leave a good impression with potential clients 46
4. Be very good to those who refer business to you 49
5. It is OK to ask for more work from satisfied clients 51
6. Make your client part of the team 53

SECTION III: AVOIDING "PROBLEM CLIENTS" AND "PROBLEM CASES"

1. On Periods of Limitations 58
2. Don't be the last link in a chain of lawyers 60
3. How to spot some warning signs of a troublesome client 62
4. Warning: The unknown client who seeks to retain you without a referral 65
5. Warning: The too-good-to-be-true client 67
6. The pluses and minuses of having a big marquee client 70
7. "I would rather pay you than pay him" 76
8. A matter of principle versus *principal,* Part 1 78
9. A matter of principle versus *principal,* Part 2 84

SECTION IV: BUILDING A GOOD REPUTATION HELPS BUILD YOUR PRACTICE

1. When a client calls…answer 88
2. Be known as a *practical* practitioner 90
3. The human element of being a lawyer and advocate 94
4. On reputation, Part 1 96
5. On reputation, Part 2 98
6. The "black shoe" lawyer 101

(Cont'd.)

SECTION V: RETAINERS AND BILLING THAT WORK FOR YOU

1. The importance of clear retainers 104
2. Difficulties with contingency case retainers 106
3. Some cautions on contingency case retainers 109
4. Billings: Make them detailed and clear 111
5. Billing: Pay attention to what your client is billed 114
6. To bill, or not to bill, office overhead charges 116
7. The importance of a non-engagement letter 118

SECTION VI: PRACTICAL ADVICE ON PRACTICING LAW

1. The secret to effective advocacy 122
2. Lead don't follow; be an advocate 125
3. Attorneys of all stripes 127
4. Beware the Law of Holes 129
5. Attend court conferences 131
6. A time to fight and a time to deal 134
7. A caution on taping calls and conversations 136

SECTION VII: PREPARING FOR TESTIMONY AND MATTERS OF THE COURTROOM

1. Our adversary system 140
2. Trial skills and the value of settlements 142
3. Loose lips sink ships 144

4. Your client as a witness 146
5. Judges are just people, too 147
6. Preparing the client for deposition testimony 148
7. Depositions: Some tricks of the trade 154
8. Getting ready for a trial, arbitration, or hearing 156
9. On direct examination 159
10. Some cautions about direct testimony 161
11. Preparing the client for cross-examination 164

SECTION VIII: COMMENTS ON DRAFTSMANSHIP

1. Write simply and clearly 168
2. Mistakes: They happen, so learn from them 171
3. Drafting relevant agreements and pleadings 173
4. Your pleadings should "bleed" a little 175
5. Responsive pleadings: make them relevant (and accurate) 178
6. On using summary judgment 181
7. An Op Ed: The obsession with conflicts of interest 185

Epilogue 189

APPENDIX

1. A sample retainer agreement 192
2. In their own words: the best & worst clients 195

Author's Biography 200

Introduction

To this day, even though law schools are designed to educate and prepare students to become lawyers, they fail to adequately teach would-be lawyers about what I call the real issues that lawyers face every day of the week. And they do a particularly poor job of informing future practitioners about running an actual law practice; getting and keeping clients; what to expect when dealing with actual clients, adversaries and judges; and what steps one can take to resolve, or at least ameliorate, the problems that will inevitably arise during your career.

While it is encouraging to see that law schools are finally implementing programs on "lawyering skills", clear, practical advice (particularly in the area of client relations) is still hard to come by. As a result, too many young lawyers harbor too many misconceptions and largely remain unprepared for practice.

I started out as a criminal prosecutor, and for the last thirty-plus years have been practicing as a commercial and construction lawyer, mainly as a litigator. So, this book has been crafted from that perspective. By that, I mean it relates to, and refers to, situations that attorneys involved in business disputes, conflict resolution, negotiations, and litigation, will no doubt deal with at some point in their careers.

One thing is certain in this profession, if you are going to really succeed as a lawyer, you will want and need to build a solid base of clients that are as loyal to you as you are to them. Satisfied clients are the best source of business for any law practice, large or small. And no amount of advertising, marketing, or public relations will ever generate more new business for you than happy clients who refer business to you. So, mainly, I will endeavor here to provide you with some time-tested strategies and methods for building a strong roster of clients.

And here is something you can take to the bank:

If you're going to have a career in law, you will make mistakes ...no matter how hard you try not to. Everyone does; you can count on it. In fact, my original title for this book was *"Practice Never Makes Perfect"* (maybe that's why they call law a *practice*). Still, I know of no good reason why anyone should make the very same mistakes that I, or other lawyers I know, have made. So, I share with you how to spot those problems before they befall you, too. My goal is to make the road you are on a smoother one than the one I have traveled.

ROBERT LESSER, ESQ.
AUGUST, 2016

Preface
LAWYERING IS A PROFESSION AND A BUSINESS BUILT ON CLIENTS

Lawyering is not about making as much money as you can (or at least it shouldn't be). And it shouldn't be all about you, or about blowing your own horn as loud and as long as you can. Lawyering is about learning to understand your client's desires, needs, strengths and weaknesses, and weaving it all into a plan that helps them achieve the results they seek.

But if you provide little or no counsel of any real value to your client; if you care about yourself more than your client; and if you do not care to become a champion of their cause, you will start out...and remain...a poor advocate. That, in turn, will not help your business. To get and retain clients, you have to be able to build a rapport with your clients and produce results for clients. These two key points are cornerstone of building a good reputation, one which will lead to referrals, and referrals are the single best source of new business for any lawyer.

Section I
INTERVIEWING AND SIGNING UP CLIENTS

1
LAWYERING IS A SERVICE BUSINESS

CONDUCT YOUR PRACTICE IN A WAY THAT CLIENTS FEEL YOU CARE ABOUT THEIR TIME AND BUSINESS AS MUCH AS THEY DO

As lawyers, we cannot ignore that we are in a service business. To have a successful service business, you have to constantly be mindful of the level of service you are providing. And a large part of that service is making sure that you have clear and consistent communication with your clients.

Too many attorneys believe that sending monthly bills is sufficient communication. It isn't. Merely sending out bills and invoices (even very detailed ones) is no substitute for human interaction, conversation, and written correspondence. So, what is it that keeps lawyers from treating their practice as the service business it is?

Well, for one thing, too many attorneys think of themselves as *The Professional*, somewhere above the mere mortal businessman. This, in part, explains why it often takes several messages left for lawyers before they will return a call or email. In other cases, there are attorneys who prefer to be ensconced in their elegant wood-and-glass paneled offices, and who believe that if a client wants to sit down and discuss an issue, the client should make an appointment and come to see *The Lawyer*. And then there are the attorneys who feel so pressed for time that even though the intent is there to return client messages promptly, something of greater urgency always comes up ... and another day passes with the ever-growing messages left unreturned.

If you recognize early in your career that you are in a

"service" profession, you will be the attorney who has no problem telling clients, *"I would be glad to come to your office to discuss your matter."* You will be amazed how much that simple act is appreciated. Your visit signals to the client that their time and effort running their business, and their lives, are as important to you as managing your own business.

It also communicates that you are, and always will be, there for them.

When you visit the client, you also place yourself in *their* environment, physically becoming part of their lives and workplace (and chances are the records, papers and documents that help your client describe his problems are located there). In addition, by making a personal visit, you have the opportunity to see your client's operation in action, and will likely meet other important personnel in the client's business. These people will get to know you, and see you as a trusted player in their business (or the boss wouldn't have asked you there). You are there with them, working on *their* issues. They come to trust you, and the more comfortable they become with you, they are more likely to call you when there are issues that they believe should be discussed with a lawyer.

The lesson here?

Run your cases and matters in a way that conveys to the client that you care about their time and business as much as they do; indeed, as much as you care about your own business. Never forget the importance of "being there", and of clear communication.

It is so easy to keep the client informed of what you are doing for him and what is the current status of his matter. All one needs to do is pick up the phone, or send an email. Do this consistently as part of your regular routine, and your reputation for being the lawyer who really does place a priority on the client's interests will grow. Your clients will appreciate you, and appreciative clients call upon you more frequently. And... *happy clients feel comfortable referring others to you.*

2
CHOOSING CLIENTS WITH CARE

BEFORE YOU SIGN A CLIENT, ASK TO SEE THE "PAPER TRAIL" OF THE EVENTS THAT LED TO THE CLIENT CALLING YOUR OFFICE.

All lawyers want clients who can pay, and who have a problem or problems to resolve. But whether you're in a small or midized practice—or if you're trying to establish your own practice—what you need to learn is how to differentiate the client who *has* a problem from the client who *is* a problem.

Determining one from the other is an ongoing process, and the dilemma besets every practicing lawyer at one time or another.

The question is: Are you the attorney who wants this person as his or her client? The answer is not always "yes". In fact, here's my prediction: One day you will get a call from someone who tells you they need an attorney. You'll ask a few questions, and you'll learn that there is a case already pending involving this person ... or worse, you might learn that a judgment has already been entered against him. This person will claim that he was never served with proper notice of the suit, or he will offer some other excuse as to why a judgment was wrongfully entered against him and why the other guy is actually the person who owes him money.

How to proceed?

You will want to know (make that *need* to know) all the facts about what transpired that led that person to call you. And if there is a history, you will want to not only hear the client's version of the facts, you will want to learn the "other side of the story" as well. Before you sign on to be anyone's lawyer, you have to ask questions. Ask to see the "paper trail" of the events leading

SECTION I: NTERVIEWING AND SIGNING UP CLIENTS / 17

up to the client calling your office. Ask your potential client what the "other guy" would say if he were present. The information you get upon such inquiries is more important than I can express. Why? Because there are all kinds of potential clients in this world, and your job (and your life) will be made so much more palatable if, at the outset, you know as much as you can about the matter before you decide whether to take on the client sitting before you.

3
THE ATTORNEY-CLIENT PRIVILEGE

ATTORNEY-CLIENT PRIVILEGE PROMOTES OPEN AND HONEST COMMUNICATIONS...THAT IS, IF THE CLIENT GIVES YOU A FULL, HONEST RECITATION OF THE FACTS.

Everyone has heard about the "attorney-client privilege". But what is it really?

In essence, the rule says that anything a client—or potential client—tells an attorney while seeking legal advice (and what the attorney tells the client in response) must be kept completely confidential. Except in rare circumstances, no one can compel the lawyer or the client to reveal what was discussed (unless the client waives the privilege).

In theory, attorney-client privilege promotes open and honest communications by a client, thus allowing you to learn all the "true" facts that brought the client to seek your advice in the first place. But no matter what you were told by other, more experienced attorneys—or by your law school professors— clients seldom tell a stranger (even their own lawyer) a full, honest recitation of the facts. So, the attorney-client privilege rarely achieves its goal of fostering open, truthful communication (although it works wonders by completely frustrating adversaries who may be desperate for information about your client when you figure out some way to keep some statement or document out of your adversary's hands by asserting the privilege).

One last word on attorney-client privilege: I suggest you make a call to any other attorney(s) with whom your potential client consulted before seeking you out on the matter at hand. While the other attorney(s) may balk at discussing details of the communications between lawyer and client, they are free to advise you of whatever impressions they formed about the client and the cause in issue. I am not saying that one should ever accept such impressions or conclusions wholesale, but those statements will give you more information on which to form your own conclusions about the case and the client.

Getting more information on which to base your next step is never a bad thing; it can only help.

4
THE INITIAL CLIENT INTERVIEW

THERE ARE AT LEAST TWO SIDES TO EVERY STORY; IT DEPENDS ON THE NUMBER OF PEOPLE TELLING THEIR VERSION OF EVENTS.

Unless you already have a long and trusting relationship with a particular client, where the client trusts you with the "truth" as he knows it, the person sitting opposite you is going to tell you his or her version of the "facts". You are going to hear the story that the client wants you to believe in the hope that you will then take that version of the "facts" and promote that story for him or her. Clients do this for many reasons, but I believe it is mainly because they want to convince themselves of what the "truth" is, and they believe that an attorney presenting those facts for them makes their story acceptable and more credible.

In the initial client interview, and later, you have to listen to a client's story with a very critical ear. If you have not learned this yet, the old saying that "there are two sides to every story" is actually dead wrong. *There are two sides to every story only if there are just two people telling their version of it.* But as any police officer, judge, detective or lawyer with any degree of "real world" experience will confirm, there are as many sides to a story as there are people who are re-telling something each saw or experienced. So, it's vitally important that you fully understand your client's version of the story from the outset.

When interviewing any client with whom you have not yet developed a long and trusting relationship, your job is not just to be a note-taker. You do not want to just take the client's version of the facts as the gospel truth. If you do, and you ultimately decide to represent this person, you will find out (and generally too late), that other people will swear things did not happen the way your client told you. If you are a litigation attorney and your client has a dispute or problem that needs to be resolved, you know that one day someone whose job it is to destroy your client's version of the events will try to take apart your client's "facts", and they will do that successfully if the "facts" related to you are not backed up by other credible people or other evidence such as contemporaneous documents. Better that you get as close to the real "facts" as early as possible than to learn them for the first time at a deposition, or at a court hearing, thanks to your adversary.

So, my suggestion is that you test the story you are being told right at the outset; not as an adversary, and not in any way that might make the client think that you do not believe him. You want to hear the details, but you want to draw them out with tact—and with well-thought out questions. You want your client to perceive you not as someone who is dubious of the story, but as someone who is thorough, and who wants to understand the entire story so you can better assist him.

The best device I have found for this is repetition.

Let your client tell his full story from start to finish with little interruption. Show interest, take notes, and listen...carefully.

Then have the client repeat the story, but this time you want to question every aspect that either does not sound quite right, or seems a bit "thin".

Then ask the client to repeat the story. Yes, a third time, and take careful note of how the story differs from the one you heard the first two times.

Changes will appear in the areas that your questions probed and tested the "facts". These differences appear where weaknesses exist, and they highlight what you will have to work on with the client to get to the bottom of the events. You have to know and understand the reasons behind the weaknesses and inconsistencies in the story if you are going to help the client ultimately prevail. And as the lawyer, you must expect that a day will come when an adversary will examine your client's story under a microscope. So, from Day One (that is, if you take on the matter and allow the client to retain you), you want the client to have a clear, cogent understanding of what his "story" is.

5
JUDGING THE CLIENT AND HIS STORY

THE MORE INFORMATION YOU HAVE ABOUT THE CLIENT—AND THE MATTER THAT LED HIM TO YOUR OFFICE—THE BETTER YOUR DECISION WILL BE TO REPRESENT HIM…OR NOT.

If, out of desperation, you need to accept *any* client with *any* cause who walks through your door with a check (retainer), you must still take the time to be a little judgmental of the client and his story.

Having seen this situation develop countless times over the years, I know this: you *need* to be even a bit more than somewhat critical of your client's story at the outset. I don't mean you should cross-examine your client, but you should try to get to a point where you can reach a solid conclusion about whether the client is right or wrong, is being completely truthful, or whether he truly believes he was wronged in some way. You need to judge both your client's claim as well as the nature of the client you are taking on. Is this person credible, sufficiently articulate, presentable, and intelligent?

Does this person's story have the ring of truth?

Many clients are passed over by other lawyers before they come to see you. And there are many reasons why some lawyers and law firms will "take a pass". A conflict may exist, or another lawyer may believe the client is without sufficient finances to pay their bills. Still, these people may have a good case and deserve to have their story or claim prosecuted on their behalf, or aired in a court of law. Take a few minutes to ask the client whether he has been to see other attorneys before you. What happened in those meetings? Why didn't your client stick with that lawyer or law firm? A client will not always respond truthfully to such questions, but how they deal with the questions may provide additional information on which to base your decision as to whether you will take on this client and his cause.

If you have a personal relationship with one of the firms—or attorneys—that your potential client met with before you, call them, especially if you have a gut feeling that something is not "adding up". Even though some information may be privileged, you still might hear something of value, or learn something that the client "forgot" to tell you. In all events, the more information you have about the client and the matter that led him to your office, the better your decision will be.

6
HELPING THE CLIENT IDENTIFY THE REAL PROBLEM

A CLIENT WHO CAN'T DEFINE HIS OWN GOALS WILL USUALLY END UP QUESTIONING WHAT YOU HAVE ACCOMPLISHED FOR HIM.

The one thing most attorneys never ask clients, at any time, let alone during the getting-to-know-you stage, is this: *"What are your goals for this matter? What do you hope to achieve by bringing or defending this action...or sending this letter...or making this offer?"*

Clarifying the client's goal(s) is the only way I know to allow you to actually help the client. So many times when you first meet a client they are driven by emotions rather than any clear goal or rational "end". In addition to whatever you might tell them, make sure you ask something like this: *"Exactly what do you want or hope to achieve by engaging me?"* and, *"What would you consider a successful outcome to be if I take on this matter"*?

These two simple questions help to focus the client on what it is he is really after.

Let me give you a few examples:

Years ago, a good client came to me complaining that a competitor "stole" one of his company's key employees. My client wanted to sue, but mainly he was driven by revenge. After a long discussion about the legal remedies available, it was clear he did not want the employee back. Nor did he want his former employee to be fired; he simply wanted to cause his competitor a lot of aggravation and expense defending a law suit, as well as to teach him a lesson not to hire any more of his employees. My point is that no lawyer should ever commence a lawsuit simply to cause the other side to spend money.

When you draft and file a complaint, that complaint had better set forth a viable cause of action of some kind or other. Otherwise, it may be you who ends up spending a lot of money if it is determined that you commenced a frivolous lawsuit and sanctions are imposed against you...not your client.

Another example:

This involved a client who purchased a large, expensive piece of equipment. The seller promised delivery by a certain date so that my client could begin producing his products. Delivery, though, was delayed more than once. My client was steaming mad, and wanted to compel delivery...and soon. But what he wanted most was the equipment and not the rancor and lawsuits that might have permanently delayed the desired delivery. So, in this case, the solution was not to sue anyone or write threatening letters. The solution rested in reaching out to help the supplier resolve certain problems that was causing delays in the manufacturing process.

There are many other such examples that I could list here. But I will refer to only one other scenario: A contractor promises completion of a home renovation by a certain date so that a family can move into their new home and enroll their kids in school. But the deadline passes, and the renovation is nowhere near complete. And on...and on...and on.

My point is that emotions run high in these kinds of cases, and emotions—not rational thought—drive how many disputes are initially viewed and addressed when cooler heads would likely lead to a clearer (and better) course of action, compromise, or resolution that would be better for all concerned.

It is up to you to explain to the client what a lawyer can and cannot do for him under the then-prevailing circumstances, and why that is. You also have to prepare the client for what options are, or may be, available to him. You also have to explain the cost in time and money, as well as the ramifications of each course. Take the time to explain to the less-sophisticated clients what is involved, and what the approximate cost will be to undertake and to pursue the plan you are formulating. Discuss whether court intervention will be needed, and what will be needed to prepare for meetings or hearings. Or, if your client is already being sued, or has been threatened with a suit, discuss what actions can be taken to avoid the suit, or to how best prepare to defend it or resolve it.

When you allow emotions to drive decisions, bad decisions often result.

In my experience, a client will appreciate your making him take a good hard look at what you can achieve together and at what cost. Of course, sometimes clients might interpret your counsel as trying to talk them out of the case...or out of your office. If that does occur, you may have lost yourself a client, but it may also prove to be the best thing that happens to you. A client who cannot define his goals will usually end up questioning what you, the lawyer, have accomplished for him.

7

THINGS THE CLIENT HAS TO BE TOLD

BE HONEST WITH THE CLIENT... TELL IT LIKE IT IS.

I never want to paint a "doom-and-gloom" scenario unless a client's case is simply one of those that has no legal basis on which to prevail. If that is the case, you will want to explain to the client—*before they spend a lot of money*—that the law is not on their side, and that winning is almost impossible if the facts are as he or she related them to you.

This is consistent with my advice in this book to be honest with the client: Tell it like it is.

One example of this occurred not so long ago in my office.

The client was terminated from his place of employment and he thought that the reason he was fired was that his boss simply didn't like him. But this client had no written contract, and no promise of continued employment. He was what many states refer to as an "at-will" employee (a term that means that the employee can be terminated for any reason at all; even for no reason). Yes, there are certain narrow circumstances where even an "at-will" employee can be wrongfully terminated (for reasons of race, religion, or disability, among others). But this client had no such issues. If he was fired because his manager did not like him, his firing was not actionable.

If, in such circumstances, you are going to help your client at all, you will be trying to get him a severance payment, or some other benefits that he would not otherwise be legally entitled to just because, for example, he was a good worker, or that he harmed no one, or that he did his job, or that losing his job would be a real hardship. In short, you would be appealing to the employer's humanity, not simply hurling empty legal threats.

Even where you do have some strong legal basis to challenge the termination—and your odds of winning do improve if you have a solid legal argument—there is still no guarantee of any particular result. The client has to know that the law, and the legal process is not pure logic, and that neither follow any hard and fast mathematical rules. That "B" does not necessarily follow "A", and that factors beyond your control, and beyond your client's control, can spoil even the best of plans.

Trust me, it will be the factors that you can exert some control over that will gnaw at you when even they go as planned.

Here is a personal example:

I had a case that by all rights should have yielded a great result monetarily for my client. We had a strong case on the facts, and we went to trial and won a large judgment. Like any complex case in New York, the process took years to make its way through the system. During those many years, our adversary cautioned his client that things could go bad. So, the defendant in our suit proceeded to wind down his company *during* the case, leaving very little by way of company assets at the end. Unlike most people, who think simply starting a new business and transferring assets into it from the old business will protect their assets (generally, Debtor-Creditor statutes prevent that very sort of conduct), the defendant in our matter was well-counseled and did most everything "by the book". In short, the defendant sold, used, or transferred company assets (i.e., from the company defendant) "for fair value", and he used up those and other assets as the business wound down over a period of years.

My client was actually awarded a fairly large judgment, and some of it was collected...but the majority of it was not. While another suit alleging fraud was instituted by another attorney for this same client, those efforts failed to recover any additional monies for the client.

So, here is a fact you should know:

No one in this country is under a mandate to keep their business open or to preserve assets for a plaintiff. What a defendant cannot do, however, is to transfer assets to others for less than fair value while a lawsuit is pending against it. That is a *de facto* fraud on creditors.

So, your client should appreciate early in the relationship that, while a money judgment is valid for 20 years (more or less, depending on the jurisdiction), unless you are suing some very large or deep pocketed entity or person, collecting any judgment might prove difficult or impossible, particularly if the party you are suing has little or no money at the time the judgment is obtained. In fact, a plaintiff is sometimes better off giving a defendant an incentive to stay in business. This can be done by making a deal early and giving the defendant an incentive to stay in business and to pay off the obligation owed to your client over time. Obtaining a large judgment against a defendant may also force a defendant to file bankruptcy. If that happens, it is no victory for your client if he sought to recover money damages, and not mere vindication of his claim. In other words, clients should know that winning, or even settling, a lawsuit for money damages is only half the battle. Collecting your judgment is the other half, and sometimes collecting is beyond difficult, or proves outright impossible.

I know some lawyers will undertake searches, or hire private investigators, to see if they can determine whether collection of a judgment will be likely or possible, assuming there is a win—or favorable settlement—for the client. I cannot say this is a good course to follow, but I also cannot say that it is not. First of all, a contested dispute can take years to make its way through the courts, and a lot of things can change in that time. Second, if a defendant is opposing the case, there is some logic to concluding that if they are defending, they have "something to lose" if they lose. Third, asset-investigation is not a precise science, and it is expensive. In the end, this is another subject to discuss with the client if you believe that you are faced with one of those matters where collection—even after a "win"—will be difficult.

8
DON'T OVER-PROMISE AS A WAY TO SIGN A NEW CLIENT

CLIENTS WHO BELIEVE YOU'VE BEEN HONEST WITH THEM ARE THE CLIENTS THAT KEEP COMING BACK...AND WHO ARE MORE INCLINED TO REFER OTHERS TO YOU.

In one of my prior firms, I used to have a partner, who I will call Dave. When conducting interviews of prospective clients, Dave would tell them whatever he believed they wanted to hear. And, if he was interested in taking them on, he invariably told them they had a "great case", and that together they were going to "wipe up" the other side. If, after many months and many dollars spent, things did not pan out as Dave predicted, he would explain all the many reasons *why* things did not go as predicted. Not one of the reasons, I assure you, involved the client's or the lawyer's shortfalls, or lack of preparation. No, the blame was always laid at the feet of a third party: the Judge, the adversary, a particularly poor witness, or even the jurors. Dave's kind of "selling" a client (call it irrational optimism) is great for signing up clients, but it's not very good for building trust or long-term relationships.

What builds trust between a lawyer and his client is open and honest on-going dialogue—about the law, life, and, of course, the case. The fact is: Not every client has "a great case".

In my own practice, even if I am completely confident that my client has a good case, I always tell the client that the legal system—like life in general—offers no guarantees. *I explain that bad results do happen in good cases,* and that is one good reason why every state in the union has appellate courts. I do, however, also say that it is far more typical that "justice" (measured by getting a fair outcome) is achievable in most matters. In the end, I have found that the clients who believe you have been honest with them from the start are the clients that keep coming back, and who are more inclined to refer others to you. Most people appreciate reasonable "straight talk".

9
WHEN YOU DON'T LIKE THE CLIENT

REPRESENTING SOMEONE YOU DON'T LIKE FROM THE START WILL LEAD TO REGRET.

There is a strong probability that if you don't like your client it is because

a. He is a creep;
b. He consistently says inappropriate things in meetings or in front of others;
c. He tells obvious falsehoods in front of others who know better;
d. He unnecessarily threatens people in meetings meant to resolve problems;
e. He acts like an obnoxious ass in front of others; or
f. He consistently lies to you, or fails to follow through on promises.

For lack of a better term, I refer to such clients as "oily" or "greasy", even though they may be perfectly well-groomed (and even if they are paying you). Oil and grease tends to spread and stain, as anyone knows who ever worked under the hood of a car. In the same way, the *behaviors* of the "oily" or "greasy" client can rub off on you. Sure, you are "just" the lawyer, but if you are seen often enough defending the actions of this sort of client, you may become the person perceived as oily and greasy over time. After awhile, others may see little difference between your client and you. And be warned: If you do represent an oily or greasy client—someone who is also a thief and a liar—that client will lie to you just as easily as he lies to others. Of course, even the worst of the worst deserve good legal representation, particularly in the criminal arena. But there, criminal defense counsel are expected to be at their best when defending the worst; it is a badge of honor of sorts. But, in my view, this does not translate well to civil litigation—particularly business and commercial disputes.

My advice: You will do yourself, your firm, and your reputation, the most good if you separate yourself from the oily or greasy client. Instead, establish rapport with your client, other lawyers, and Judges, and develop a reputation for being a person of his or her word. That is time better spent than trying to explain away the indefensible or reprehensible conduct of the "oily" client.

10

FOR SOME CLIENTS, JUST SAY "NO"

YOUR INSTINCTS ARE OFTEN YOUR GREATEST ASSET, SO LEARN TO SAY "NO" REGARDLESS OF HOW HUNGRY YOU ARE FOR BUSINESS.

When your gut tells you that something in your client's story is wrong, or if you have an uneasy feeling about the client, you may live to regret taking on this particular client or matter. So, learn to say "no" regardless how hungry you are for business.

As a lawyer, or just as a thinking, intelligent being, your instincts are often your greatest asset. Let them guide you, because if something seems amiss before you even hear the "other" side of the story, something likely is amiss. And, if some day you do find you've gotten involved in a case you deeply regret, there are usually ways to extricate yourself from such situations...but they take time and effort. And it's always easier to not get involved in a matter *before* it starts.

Here's another reason to just say "no":

Lawyers' fees based on hourly charges can add up fast. And many lawyers will spend much of their time working for clients who are constantly indebted to them because they are not timely paying their lawyer's bills. Every month that goes by unpaid, or underpaid, only makes the debt grow larger. Most of us don't want to let go of a client that owes us a good deal of money, because sometimes the only hope of getting paid what we're owed (or a good piece of it) is to hang in with the client. But remember this: No matter how well you perform for some clients—unless you produce a good pot of money for them by way of settlement or judgment, so that you can pay yourself what you are owed before sending them the last bill—your payday may never come.

I speak from a wealth of experience on this issue.

If you ever face the indebted client problem, you will surely be promised payment in full. The client will say things like, *"I'll pay you soon"*, or, *"You're the last person on earth I would stiff; I mean, come on, you? My lawyer?"* But more often than not when clients owe you large sums for services already rendered, the words may be well-intentioned, but they are hollow. If, for whatever reason, you are unable to generate a recovery from which you can be paid, you might well be the last person that your client "stiffs", but you *will* be stiffed.

So if you do find yourself in the unenviable position of being owed a large sum of money, and that sum keeps growing, ignore the praise your client bestows on you. Ignore, too, the promises of payment that will be repeated in many forms over and over (sometimes accompanied by small sums of money that do little to pay down the debt owed), and advise the client to find another attorney. *Graciously and professionally resign from the representation, and advise the client that you expect to be paid for the services rendered.*

If there is an action pending in which you have appeared as attorney of record, you will likely need to be formally "substituted out of the case" by a new lawyer. Or, you will have to ask the Court for leave to be relieved as counsel. This requires a motion made on notice to your client. Thankfully, more and more courts are granting such motions upon a showing that the lawyer is suffering a hardship ... or that the client has breached his obligations under the retainer agreement ... or that a rift in the attorney-client relationship has been caused that will work to the detriment of the client, and lawyer.

But remember, the longer you have been in the case, and the closer the matter is to actual trial, the more difficult it will be to have the Court let you out of a pending case. So do not let the matter linger. I have to assume that you have better things to do with your time than to be locked into a case where you have ill feelings for the client and find yourself preparing a case for no fee.

Section II
STRATEGIES FOR EXPANDING YOUR CLIENT BASE

1
TURNING NON-CLIENTS INTO CLIENTS

NOT EVERY CALLER BECOMES A NEW CLIENT. BUT TRY TO MAKE SURE YOU LEAVE EVERY PERSON WHO REACHES OUT TO YOU FEELING THAT YOU'RE INTERESTED IN THEM AND IN THEIR WELFARE.

Referrals are a large part of most attorneys' business. So, when someone calls me and says, "*I was referred to you by . . .*" I make time, I listen, and I find a few minutes to try to engage in easy conversation, even if it becomes clear to me that the matter being discussed is not my specialty, or perhaps presents an irreconcilable conflict, or perhaps it's something I am not interested in accepting.

Not every caller becomes a new client, of course. But I try to make sure I leave every single person who reaches out to me with the impression that I'm interested in *them* and in their welfare. Because, at the end of the call, I want them to hang up the phone thinking that I can be trusted to come back to if necessary. And even if I cannot help them on this matter, I let them know I can refer them to someone else who can. Also, I try to follow up such a conversation with an email a few weeks later, asking if things are being handled appropriately, and inviting them to feel free to reach out to my firm again if anything else needs an attorney's attention.

Once again, you are reminding a potential client that you care about what happened to them. But even that kind of outreach should not be the end of your involvement with the non-client.

If you are going to refer someone to another lawyer, I have two suggestions:

First, only refer a matter to an attorney who you trust to have the right skill-set and is the right person to handle the matter in a quality manner. You never want to have someone come back with a complaint like, "*Why did you send me to that guy? He ran me in circles, accomplished nothing, and cost me a bundle, too!*"

Second, follow up with a call to the lawyer to whom you referred the matter. It only has to be a brief, friendly call; one professional to another. A simple, "*How did it go?*" will do the trick. By this, you accomplish two things: You've reminded that lawyer that it was you who referred the matter, and, hopefully, this will lead to a return of the favor.

By having these short discussions, you create dialogue, which is how relationships and trust begin to take root. Also, having such conversations (and not just one where you said something like, "*Call Joe Smith*"), the client is likely to feel more comfortable calling you the next time. The idea is to impress the client that you care about them and/or his business, for which they may call you again. Put metaphysically, you could say that the good karma will come back to you (or what goes around comes around). Of course, this is not always true. But it takes so little effort, and eventually you will see positive results by making it a consistent and valuable part of your work ethic.

2
KEEPING YOUR NAME AT THE TOP OF YOUR CLIENT'S MIND

DEVELOP WAYS OF KEEPING YOUR NAME IN FRONT OF EXISTING AND PAST CLIENTS, AS WELL AS THOSE PEOPLE WHO REFERRED BUSINESS TO YOU IN THE PAST.

A person looking for a lawyer is more likely to call the attorney whose name is at the top of his mind. So, it's important that you develop ways of keeping *your* name in front of existing and past clients, as well as in front of those who have referred business to you in the past.

Some lawyers accomplish this by distributing "swag", those inexpensive giveaways (pens, business card holders, key chains, etc.) imprinted with their firm name, address and telephone number. They're good to hand out to anyone who stops in the office, or to be left at accountants' offices, cafes, dental offices, and just about any place where people gather who may need a lawyer.

Other lawyers (like yours truly), prefer to send targeted email messages, or notes, attaching news articles that I believe are relevant and of interest to a particular client. Not infrequently, a client will call and thank me, and tell me how timely the article was. In that way, for the moment at least, I not only put myself at the "top of mind" to that client, but he understands that even though I might not be engaged in any active matters for him right then, I still have his interests in mind. Another marketing tool with the same purpose is so obvious that I wondered if I should even mention it.

But here goes:

Often, I will send a simple, friendly hello by email to suggest that the client, or other possible referrer of business, and I make lunch or dinner plans.

Even if their response is something like, "*Sure, let's do that soon . . .*", such communications keep my name in front of the client and builds on a relationship that might otherwise become estranged or "lost" over time. I do this for another reason as well: I totally enjoy being with many of my clients and contacts. In many instances we have also become friends.

Of course, many big law firms draft monthly newsletters for their large institutional clients. Personally, I don't believe these nonspecific newsletters offer much value for firms serving smaller clientele. And in any event, most solo or small firms don't have the time to research, write, print, and disseminate newsletters. And yet, there is an easy way to test whether this form of marketing is right for you: There are many marketing companies that create generic legal newsletters. They will brand any communique you select with your firm's name and logo, and they'll even mail them for you. At some of these firms, you can even select the topics and layout you prefer, and target the "news" to your client base as best you can. If you think this method will help your practice, you can try it out for a small investment. After all, it only takes one good new retainer to make the entire mailing worth the effort and cost.

Here's the bottom line: When a person is in need of an attorney, it is very helpful if the name of *your* law firm is staring right up at him from his desk.

3
LEAVE A GOOD IMPRESSION WITH POTENTIAL CLIENTS

IF YOU DON'T MAKE A PERSONAL, ONE-ON-ONE IMPRESSION ON POTENTIAL CLIENTS, YOU'VE SQUANDERED AN OPPORTUNITY.

What would do you do if a potential new client reached out to you by phone, and described a legal problem that you knew could be addressed simply and easily?

Well, I'll tell you what I've done in the past...but what I do no longer.

In the past, I felt compelled to impart some knowledge over the phone that I knew could help, hoping that by leaving a good impression I would be called if that individual needed further help. Of course, this tactic is great for the potential client (especially if you solve their issue in a single phone call)...but it is not so great for your business. Because the person you were able to assist so quickly probably won't remember that it was you who handed him a relatively easy, and remarkably quick, solution to his problem.

Making lasting impressions on potential clients takes more than just being a nice guy, or being the person with a fast...even correct...answer to the problem presented.

I'll illustrate with a personal example:

A few years ago, I received a referral from a lawyer friend. The caller said a neighbor had closed off a dirt road access to commercial property he recently purchased, preventing his trucks from accessing his office and warehouse. In that very first (and *only*) call, I learned that he had purchased the property for his business, and needed that truck access, or he would not have bought the land and buildings in the first place. After some discussion about the transaction and his access rights to and from his property (and thinking "easement"), I asked whether he recalled purchasing title insurance at the time he bought the property. He said he had. I then explained that his title insurance company should be notified immediately as they might well have the obligation to defend his right of access, and possibly prosecute the matter, if necessary, on his behalf ... all without a cost to him.

I assume that everything we discussed in that one call proved true, as I never heard from the caller again. And my lawyer friend, who suggested the individual call me in the first place, also never heard from the person about the matter. Now, I would be willing to bet that that potential client cannot even recall that it was I with whom he spoke and who presented him—on that first call—with that simple solution.

From a business standpoint, a far better outcome might have resulted if I had resisted my temptation to fix his problem on the phone. If, instead, I had asked the caller to come in and sit down, or simply to send me his papers and documents from the closing, I would have given myself the opportunity to discuss things face-to-face, or to have some correspondence, and then confer with him later at greater length and depth regarding title policy and his rights in general. In this way, the caller would have had my letterhead and card; everything he would need to re-contact me in the future.

The experience taught me an important lesson:

If you don't make a personal, one-on-one impression on a potential client (even if you never meet face-to-face), you have squandered an opportunity to develop the start of a solid client relationship. Even if you offer a solution that is quick, free, and painless, the client now knows you. And *that* is a client who *will* remember you, and will return if he has issues in the future.

Don't let potential clients simply walk out of your life.

Make an impression.

Give them something by which to remember, whether it's a friendly discussion, a business card, or some level of attention to their problem that says you're there to help.

4
BE VERY GOOD TO THOSE WHO REFER BUSINESS TO YOU

IF AN ATTORNEY REFERS ONE OF HIS CLIENTS TO YOU, ALWAYS LET THAT ATTORNEY KNOW THAT YOU WON'T TRY TO MAKE THAT CLIENT YOUR CLIENT FOR ALL TIME, AND THAT YOU WILL "RETURN" THEM.

As your practice grows, some people inevitably will call and say, "*I was referred to you by so-and-so*".

When that happens, send a friendly email, or make a phone call to the referrer to extend your thanks. Tell them how much you appreciate the gesture, and that you will let them know whether you and the referred party are going to work together or not. And, as I suggested earlier, make it a point to meet anyone referred to you that sounds like they might have business that you can handle ...even if you have a strong inclination not to take on the matter. You always want to give yourself an opportunity to leave your mark with a potential client. After all, future business may flow directly or indirectly from that person, or from someone they refer to you. Besides, you owe it to any person who drops your name to make that person look good whether you end up taking on the matter or not.

Typically, a referrer will be a client, another lawyer, or a person in a profession that routinely deals with attorneys (real estate professionals, accountants, insurance brokers, etc.). So, when someone does refer a case to you, and the client proves valuable to your firm, send a personal note and thank-you gift to the person who referred the client. And, if you are ever in a position to do so, try to repay the favor in kind. In other words, refer clients to that person if you believe the "fit" is right. You never know, a real relationship may develop between you and the party who referred you to the point where people are regularly coming into, or calling, your office saying something like, "*Joe Smith said you're the best*".

It is a great situation to have, and it will only develop if you reach out to say thanks and, if appropriate to do so, to send a small gift; a reminder of how much you appreciate the referral. Believe me, lawyers, accountants, and others, all appreciate professional sports tickets, theater tickets, dinners in nice restaurants and gift cards. The one caution is to make sure the jurisdiction in which you practice allows such gift-giving, and to be careful because many jurisdictions have proscriptions against "fee-splitting" with lawyers who performed no services on a matter unless they are a member of your firm. So, you do not want to send a percentage of the fees earned or a "gift" worth thousands of dollars, nor do you need to. Your referrer will appreciate a gift on the order of what I have suggested, and to an even greater degree, will appreciate your referrals back to them.

One last word on this subject:

If an attorney refers one of his clients to you because of a conflict or some other reason that made the referrer not take the matter himself, always, I repeat, *always*, let that attorney know that you will never try to make that client *your* client for all time, and that you will "return" the client to him. If you try to make that client your own for all future matters, that news will spread quickly, and you will never get such a referral from that lawyer again (and, just as likely, not from any other attorneys he knows either).

5
IT'S OK TO ASK FOR MORE WORK FROM SATISFIED CLIENTS

YOUR CLIENT MAY NOT SEND YOU WORK JUST BECAUSE YOU ASKED FOR IT, BUT SOME CLIENTS WILL SEND YOU MORE WORK BECAUSE YOU DID.

Many years ago, one of the senior partners where I worked gave me this advice: *"Never be afraid to ask your clients for work"*.

I used to think that by doing so my clients might think less of me. But there is no shame in asking for more work from someone who already thinks well of you. And, personally, I have never heard any negative comments about my having asked, and, to my knowledge, I never lost a client because I did ask.

It is not a given that work will be sent to you simply because you asked for it, but some clients will send you more work because you asked. *It's not an act of charity; it's a function of timing.* You happened to ask at a time when the client had a present need to have a lawyer review a contract, or to give them advice on some matter or transaction, or had a pending situation. And because you spoke up, you were, as I have put it "at the top of the client's mind" when the need arose.

Here's an example of how this has worked for me:

One day, I called a client who owned a successful construction business. Like many successful and busy people, the principal had many lawyers that he turned to for different aspects of his life and business. I called this person not because I was working on something for him, but because while I dealt with him on many things, I had no open files with him at that time. I called basically to say "hi", and in that conversation I said something like, *"I was* just thinking of you because it's been a while. So, I thought I'd call and ask how things are with you. I gather things are well, as I haven't heard from you, and I guess that's good news for you. But, if anything comes up, you know where to reach me".

The call could have ended right there if he had said something like, "*Thanks for calling*" or, "*I'm too busy to talk right now*". Instead, he said something like, "*You know, as long as I have you on the phone, let me run something by you*". As it happened, he had a small dispute brewing with another contractor and he brought my firm into the matter to review the contracts in issue and to advise him on how best to proceed. Had I not made the call suggesting that he "knew where to reach me", it is just as likely that he would have addressed the issue himself, or perhaps turned to another one of his other legal advisers.

No matter what the reason is for having a client on the phone, or in your office, *use the time to highlight what you have accomplished for him as his lawyer*. More importantly, never forget to take the time to show genuine interest in the client. Ask about your client, his work, his travels, his family. After all, the practice of law isn't really about you at all; it is all about the client(s). The more the client enjoys speaking with you, the more comfortable the relationship is, the more likely it is that you will be the attorney at the top of his mind when he wants or needs to call a lawyer.

A caution, though:

I wouldn't make it a frequent habit of asking for work from any particular client(s). Once or twice may yield results, and if you *do* get work for the asking, you have now gained a reason to speak with greater frequency with the client(s) about those new matters.

6
MAKE YOUR CLIENT PART OF THE TEAM

USE YOUR CLIENT'S WILLINGNESS AND DESIRE TO HELP, PROVIDED THEIR EFFORTS WILL HELP AND NOT HINDER.

In medicine, patients put their faith and trust in their doctors, and sleep blissfully through surgery while the specialists do whatever is called for to achieve a successful outcome. In law, *the opposite is true*; we want and need a client's input and participation in order to achieve a successful outcome.

So, when taking on any new matter, explain to your clients that their involvement in a legal dispute is not like having a heart or other medical problem. From the start, we rely on our clients to tell us what the problem (or perceived problem) is. And we need them to talk to others who may have something to add to the story, and to encourage those others to be responsive to, and to assist, us in bringing about a good result for the client.

Many lawyers will tell their clients to watch what they say to anyone and to "stay out of the way"...and for some clients this is very good advice. But if you have an intelligent, knowledgeable client who wants to be involved in his matter, he can save you a lot of time, and can save himself an awful lot of money. How? Well, for example, a client with a document-intensive case, will likely know those documents far better than you ever will, and, thus, he may be in a better position to know which are important, which are not, and how best to categorize and organize them.

My advice: Use your client's willingness and desire to help, provided his efforts will help and not hinder. This advice is particularly compelling when your client is person who is an expert in his field. There are so many matters where you, as a lawyer, would have to retain an expert to help you understand the issues in a case. This happens all the time. For example, if you are dealing with a dispute involving the manner in which monies were accounted for between partners, you will need a CPA or a trained accountant to help you understand the records that form the documentary evidence in the case. If your client is an accountant, who better than they to assist in making the matter understandable for you.

Another issue that can create problems (or benefits) when you make your client part of the team concerns the subject of client-to-client contact. I am referring to whether you should allow your client to reach out to, or to continue having contact/discussions with, your adversary's client. Lawyers differ on this subject. And, while virtually every state has rules that prohibit any lawyer from having direct contact with another lawyer's client, the area of client-to-client contact is generally not regulated (although, you should always check local rules about this subject, and understand that you cannot make any third-party your agent for reaching out to your adversary's client. Put simply, you are not allowed to do indirectly what you cannot do directly).

Of course, as an attorney, you can instruct a client not to have contact with his adversary (that is, the other party to the dispute or case), and if that advice is ignored, one can turn to the Court to seek an order preventing unwanted contact between the clients if the circumstances warrant. But, in my firm, in the absence of a proscription against contact by your client, we at least consider the relative merits of having clients have contact with the adversary client where circumstances are appropriate.

In some cases, it is virtually unavoidable to have ongoing contacts (such as where the matter at hand involves members of the same extended family, or perhaps the clients share the same workplace). But in other circumstances, good things can come from two people continuing to speak, if they can treat each other civilly. In fact, over the years I have handled many matters where disputes are resolved because two individuals realize that the things they have in common outweigh whatever the dispute was that caused the dispute to arise in the first instance. If this does occur, the client will often credit you with providing the impetus for the "other guy" coming around to see the light. Whatever the cause, a settlement or resolution that pleases the client is a good thing when it happens on your watch. This is particularly true if you make the time to explain that the good result was at least in part brought about by the actions you have taken for him.

A word of caution on client-to-client communications:

As recollections about oral communications will always differ, even if only slightly, always warn a client that he should never write anything to the adversary, no matter what format (texts, emails, even pen-and-paper). Writings can last forever, and more often than not, they are not open to more than one interpretation. In my firm we also always caution clients to never say or write anything that you would not want played back in court. It is truly amazing to me what some people will say on voicemail. Such messages can prove extremely detrimental (or helpful, if it is the *other* guy who was foolish enough to make that kind of error.)

Section III
AVOIDING PROBLEM-CLIENTS AND PROBLEM CASES

1
ON PERIODS OF LIMITATIONS

WHETHER YOU TAKE ON THE CLIENT'S CAUSE OR NOT, YOU HAVE TO MAKE IT CLEAR—PREFERABLY IN WRITING—THAT ACTION IS REQUIRED WITHIN WHATEVER TIME GOVERNS.

If your client's claim is against a municipal, state or federal institution or agency, it is highly likely that a notice of claim is required under some statute governing claims against that entity.

If your client has a claim to assert, or a lawsuit to file, you have to give some thought in that very first client interview, to the issue of whether there is sufficient time left under the governing notice or claim rules, statute of limitations, or any contractual period of limitations, to commence a suit, or, if appropriate, to file a "notice of claim".

Typically, statutes provide for short time limits in notice of claim scenarios and, further, direct both how and upon whom such notices must be served. Even if you determine that you would like to take on the client, it may well be that the client has sat on his rights for too long and the claim he wanted to file is already barred. Or, it may prove out that time is critically short.

You must give consideration to these issues immediately... on Day One. Because, whether you decide to take on the client's cause or not, you have to make it clear to the client, preferably in writing, that the proverbial clock is ticking, and action is required within whatever time governs. (*See also Section V on non-engagement letters*).

The last thing you want to have happen to you is to be considered the "attorney of record" on a matter where the applicable period of limitations was "live" while you were on the case, but expired before you filed the right document (whether it's a summons and complaint or a notice of claim). Allowing that to happen is malpractice *per se*.

2
DON'T BE THE LAST LINK IN A CHAIN OF LAWYERS

THE CLIENT WHO HAS HAD SEVERAL LAWYERS ON THE SAME MATTER SHOULD BE A RED FLAG TO YOU.

A potential client comes to you with a great story about the case in which he's involved. In the course of the conversation, you learn that he has already been through two or three other law firms who actually took on the cause, but who, for one reason or another, are no longer representing him.

Whether it was the client who terminated the relationship with his attorney, or it was the law firm that signed on initially but then thought the better of it, makes little or no difference: A line of unsatisfied lawyers who represented this person on the *same* matter, or the client who found something wrong with *every* lawyer he dealt with on the same matter (or a combination of the two), should be a bright, flashing proceed-with-caution sign.

I have never, even once, experienced a situation where several prior law firms have abandoned the same client (or who were discharged by the client), where some major relational or other serious problem was not also present. So, if you can afford to say "no"...say, "no". Take a pass on the matter. I have never met the client and case with that sort of back story that worked out well for me. There was always some issue, some major issue, that caused me to regret accepting the matter. Think about it: No matter what this potential client tells you about the case, *something caused those other lawyers to seek to divorce themselves from that client, or caused the client to want to jettison the lawyer(s).* More often than not, that "something" is money; or more to the point, the lack thereof. Simply put, in most cases the client likely did not pay his lawyers as promised.

But it doesn't have to involve money.

It might be something even more important.

Perhaps the client has lied about the facts, or has, literally, made up facts or falsified documents. Or, he may have already invoked the ire of the adversary, or even the Court, in a pending case, to the point where some Order has been issued that questions his veracity... or, maybe he has been Ordered to produce some record or other evidence under threat of contempt.

Or, it could just be a simple case of "bad chemistry". You just have to trust your instincts.

Sure, it is possible that the client was just not a good fit for the other lawyer(s), and you won't have any issue with him. But my experience teaches that that result is highly unlikely, and the likelihood that I am wrong is directly disproportional to the number of lawyers (or law firms) that were previously representing the client. One more thing: If there is a promise of money up front (that is, payment of your retainer), and that promise is broken, you might wish to consider your new potential relationship to be at an early end. If you ignore this advice and take on the matter anyway, you can (and will) blame yourself for ignoring not one, but at least two back-to-back warning signs.

3
HOW TO SPOT SOME WARNING SIGNS OF A TROUBLESOME CLIENT

IF YOU FIND YOURSELF ARGUING MORE WITH—AND NOT FOR—YOUR CLIENT, IT IS TIME TO FIND AN EXIT STRATEGY FROM THE SITUATION.

Treat every client with respect no matter what...at least in the beginning.

But if your intuition tells you something might be amiss, then make it clear that you can't get involved with a case until...

a. Your retainer check is received and cleared in full;
b. You have a signed retainer letter with the terms you agree upon (don't accept retainers on any terms but your own);
c. You have, with the client's permission, contacted any prior counsel to discuss the matter.

If the client balks at you speaking with prior counsel, the problem might be worse than you thought.

In my experience, the desire by some clients that you not reach out to any previous law firm the client may have retained for the matter indicates that the law firm has little, if anything good to say, or perhaps was not paid, and is not going to be paid. If the latter is the case, it is likely that your own bills will receive similar treatment. But if you are a very hungry young lawyer, who believes he has to take the matter, then tread carefully. Write a retainer that allows you to resign from a case if promises of prompt payment are not kept. And, follow through on that if you are repeatedly promised money that never materializes, or if it does, is never in the sum you were promised. Also make it your practice to always collect a fair sum as a retainer at the outset of any new relationship.

What are some other warning signs of a troublesome client?

It is likely that this client will say he agrees with your fee rate and other retainer terms as set forth in your letter, but then asks if it's OK to send you *half* (or part) of the requested retainer sum "now" with the balance to be sent later (pick one: next week, next Tuesday, next month, next never). This sort of client may also ask you to alter the retainer agreement itself, a day or so after he just signed it. Accepting a far smaller sum than you think is appropriate, on a promise of a payment coming soon, is just the sort of vortex that sucks in lawyers.

When a new relationship begins this way, no matter how well you do for the client, no matter what miracles you may conjure or perform, you will rarely emerge financially whole (i.e., getting paid as established in the retainer). Remember this: The first sign of trouble—always—is that the client who is balking at making payment as he initially promised, has cycled through two or more lawyers or law firms before calling you for the same issue or dispute. That should be the flashing red neon sign that splits the night with a single word... "Warning".

There is still another trait inherent in some potential clients that has been a consistent indicator of trouble ahead: It's the client who, from the start, begins arguing with you over matters trivial and not-so-trivial. Remember, most clients seek out lawyers to describe their problem, and then carefully listen to and follow the advice they receive.

So, if the person sitting across from you starts the relationship by vociferously arguing with you, you are more than likely looking at a person who will not follow your advice... will continue to question the wisdom of the actions you take on his behalf (and this is after you have discussed with the client the course that should be taken)...and, no doubt, will later contest the value of the services you rendered (again, finding a reason to not pay for those services).

No matter how well you get along with others, and even if you have never had this kind of situation occur before, it is a fact that sometimes in the course of human affairs (no matter what you say or do to try to correct the situation), two people will interact like oil and water—meaning they cannot interact—at least not on any level worth tolerating for long. *Life is too short, and the practice of law is stressful enough.*

If you find yourself arguing more with—and not for—your client, it is time to find an exit strategy from the situation. Maybe that means finding another lawyer in your firm to step in, if possible. Or maybe you will need to use some other means I set out in this book. In short, find the nicest and fastest way possible to end the relationship.

4

WARNING: THE UNKNOWN CLIENT WHO SEEKS TO RETAIN YOU WITHOUT A REFERRAL

NEVER TAKE A CASE THROUGH AN UNSOLICITED FAX OR EMAIL WITHOUT FIRST CHECKING THE SOURCE BY MEANS OTHER THAN AN EMAIL BACK TO THE VERY PARTY THAT CONTACTED YOU.

We've all received unsolicited emails and faxes from some domestic or foreign business that promise to send us a breach of contract collection case. All we need do is agree to act as local counsel to send a collection letter about a large sum of money owed to the person who sent us the email or fax, or to aid them in getting some money out of some foreign country.

Most of us are savvy enough to recognize these blatant efforts as a scam or thievery. And yet... well, some of these ruses can be pretty sophisticated. They use real company names and the names of real executives at those companies. And if you search online for those names, they will show up. The treachery is usually hidden behind very subtle differences in email addresses employed by these parties. Of course, all of these scams have been crafted to get you to place money into your attorney account so that the fraudulent parties can then empty your account, or at least legitimize or "wash" money, the provenance of which would otherwise be highly suspect.

Here's how the scams work:

You will be informed that the company is owed a lot of money, and that recent efforts at collection (by others) has led to the debtor agreeing to send you a large check in settlement of the claim. Typically, you will be asked to have the check made payable to your firm, thus requiring that you deposit it into an account in your firm's name. Then, you wait for the check to clear, and the bank might actually advise you that it has cleared. Your instructions are to pay yourself a fee from the proceeds and to send (usually by wire) the balance to your "new client".

Two or three weeks later, your bank's fraud department will no doubt notify you that the check you deposited was fraudulent. Or worse, you may get a visit from the FBI advising you the money you deposited was from illegal activities of one kind or another. And if you deposited the check into an account holding other clients' funds, the money you sent to the "new client" was actually money that rightfully belonged to your *actual* clients and/or the bank's money obtained via the fraud.

What could be worse? Well, if that check was in your trust account—which you probably thought it should have been, as part or all of a settlement—you just transferred your *other* clients' monies to the thieves. I don't have to tell you that the consequences of this can be devastating to you, your firm, your reputation...not to mention to your finances and your client relationships.

Never, I repeat, *never*, take on a case that you obtained through an unsolicited lead over a fax or email without thoroughly checking the source by means *other* than an email back to the very party that contacted you in the first place. And, never give any bank account number to any party that you do not know and trust. You have more to lose than just your—or your clients'—money.

5

WARNING: THE TOO-GOOD-TO-BE-TRUE CLIENT

PROTECTION OF YOUR CLIENTS IS A NOBLE GOAL...BUT PROTECTING YOURSELF, YOUR LAW LICENSE, AND YOUR FAMILY, MUST COME FIRST OR YOU WILL BE OF NO USE TO ANYBODY.

You know that old saying, if something seems too good to be true, it probably is. Well, the cliché is no less applicable to clients.

Unfortunately, there are a lot of people making a living in the so-called "black", "grey", or other semi-legal or outright illegal markets. They sell knock-offs goods as originals, or they sell merchandise that has (oops) "fallen off a truck". And then, as part of their fraudulent enterprise, they need to find ways to make their profits un-traceable or at least less traceable. So, they often prey on lawyers—particularly young, hungry lawyers—to assist them with their "business problems".

There's nothing wrong with a lawyer taking on any client who truly needs legal advice; even outright criminals have a right to counsel. And, so long as the lawyer is actually providing legal representation services, he is entitled to be paid for the services he legitimately renders. A huge problem may be lurking, however, if your client wants you to simply call or write someone for money, and when that money comes in, to place it into your "trust" account for clearing; or worse, to open up a separate special account for them into which they can place sums of money from time to time and subsequently withdraw them.

If you are approached by such a "businessman" who claims to be owed monies but doesn't want you to actually file lawsuits or to pursue standard legal avenues to collect the monies he is owed …and he tells you that either he, or someone else, is working on the actual collections…that should cause alarm bells to go off in your head. What are you really being asked to do? Is it to simply place often large-sum checks (very often from different named companies) into your trust account, and, upon full clearance, to cut your client a check from your trust account less, say, 15 percent for yourself? Or is it simply to allow this "client" to have access to a special account you have opened for him? If either of these scenarios are present, repeat after me: money-laundering, money-laundering…*money-laundering*.

True story:

About 7 years ago, I hired a law student (I will call him Richard) to clerk at my firm. Upon graduation, we wished Richard the best of luck and wrote him a nice recommendation. We didn't hear from him for some time. Recently, Richard called me, asking if I could help him start a solo practice in New Jersey. I asked what he had been doing since we had last spoken, and he explained that getting a good law job after graduation proved to be harder than he thought. So again, I asked what he'd been doing lately. "*Oh*," he said, "*Well, I did six months in Allenwood*". For those of you not familiar with "Allenwood", it's a minimum-security federal penitentiary in Pennsylvania, mainly for non-violent offenders.

I was stunned. "*Rich, what happened?*"

He said that after looking unsuccessfully to join a firm he had been running his own law firm in the Bronx section of New York City, and was introduced to some businessmen who made him an offer he found very hard to turn down.

Basically, the arrangement proposed to him was something very close to what I described above.

Richard would make calls for money allegedly owed his clients, and the money was—quite remarkably—sent in full almost all of the time. Richard would then put the money into his trust account, after which he wrote checks back to his "clients" for most of what was collected less a small percentage for his troubles. But Richard's real troubles started when he was visited by several federal agents investigating the "businessmen" with whom Richard had become affiliated. It seems Richard had done almost no work (if any) to show for his "fees", and it turned out he had been facilitating a money-laundering operation.

In New York, and in many other jurisdictions, the law makes it quite plain that one cannot simply close their eyes to something that to a reasonable person would seem not quite right. And while you can certainly render legal advice and services to outright criminals, you cannot help them commit the crimes or avoid detection. The agents believed Rich "had to know" that what he was doing was illegal, and that made him an accessory, not a lawyer. If you are convicted of a felony in New York, it's basically a *fait accompli* that you lose your license to practice law, and Richard was disbarred in New York. Thus, his call to me about establishing a *New Jersey* practice. We had a short conversation about New Jersey requirements, and I cautioned Rich not to simply hang out a shingle, but to check with the Bar Association of New Jersey, and to make sure that he could still lawfully practice in New Jersey. He said he would do things "by the book". It has now been many months, and I have not heard from him since.

I'm telling you this story as a cautionary tale: If something seems too easy, you need to look closely...very closely. Protection of your clients is a noble goal. But protecting yourself, your law license, and your family, must come first or you will be of no use to anybody.

6
THE PLUSES AND MINUSES OF HAVING A BIG MARQUEE CLIENT

WHEN YOU HAVE A MARQUEE CLIENT, EVERY PAPER YOU FILE, AND EVERY LETTER YOU SEND ON THAT CLIENT'S BEHALF, WILL LIKELY CAUSE YOU SOME STRESS...AND THE MORE SIGNIFICANT ACTIONS WILL GENERATE EVEN MORE STRESS.

Most attorneys with a solo or small firm practice dream about "landing the big one"...getting one or two large clients (or more, if possible) who appreciate your services, appreciate you, and who pay their bills on time without a quibble. It's a great goal, but unless your family or a close friend controls a very large business and wants you to handle some of their legal work, landing and retaining The Big One is more difficult than you know.

There are at least two reasons this is so.

For one thing, large enterprises are highly structured, multi-tiered organizations, and there is the problem of identifying and reaching the decision-maker. Is it the CEO or the general counsel (or one of several or even hundreds of in-house lawyers); is it a department vice president; or just a credit manager charged with collecting a debt? Today, you can try searching the company's own website and other online sites to determine which department or person controls that decision. And, for the very determined lawyer, several well-placed phone calls into the firm might assist the search. I have heard of other lawyers attending seminars for in-house counsel, and/or for credit managers to try to get a leg up on the search. It is a lot of work, and there is no guarantee that you will ever reach the right person.

Second, even if you do successfully make your way through

the corporate maze, you will still face resistance. Corporate decision-makers are highly resistant to sticking their necks out for a small service provider. For example, back in the 1980's, when mass distribution of computers was still a young industry, it was so much easier for companies to say, *"Let's just buy IBM"* (which at the time was the largest supplier of "mini-computers" and servers in the nation) than to purchase from a smaller vendor. Because if something went wrong with the selected computer system, someone in upper management of the purchasing company might have asked, *"What genius decided to buy from Small Solutions Inc.?"* Back then, though, even if huge problems resulted from purchasing from IBM, no one got fired for deciding to buy from an established, trusted brand like IBM.

This same reasoning holds true today when it comes to businesses retaining lawyers and law firms to handle their legal problems.

Large businesses generally consider legal fees—and lawyers—to be a necessary corollary to doing business. And, while legal bills draw much greater scrutiny today than they did even the recent past, they are still processed and paid every month in virtually every large business in America. This is, at least in part, what keeps America's—indeed the world's—largest law firms busy days, nights, and weekends. So when a big, marquee company has a legal matter, the person in charge of choosing which lawyer to refer a matter to, will more often than not, pick up the phone and call one of several different large firms deemed acceptable to that company. (Large companies generally have several such approved or "go-to" law firms, depending on the kind of problem faced at the moment).

However, small law firms do have a better chance of getting work from a big enterprise *if* they can distinguish themselves as having some narrow specialty in terms of experience or knowledge that gives them a discernible edge over larger players in a particular area of law.

So, how can small law firms—even solos—get their foot in the door?

The first way is to impress on a large, well-established law firm representing such clients that you bring value to the client if you are on their team. It is not often that a large, powerful law firm will turn to a small firm for assistance...but occasionally they do. This is most often seen when retaining competent "local" counsel in a city outside of their normal jurisdiction; and, less often, to obtain expertise in a niche area in which they might not be totally comfortable. The second, and far more difficult way to get your foot in the door, is to impress on the client directly that you will accomplish as good or better results in a particular matter, *at far less cost than their usual counsel.*

This is not an easy sale to make; hiring your firm means someone is sticking their neck way out for you.

Still, if you are dogged enough (and lucky enough) to be retained, you will find that you have now landed a demanding client that keeps you extremely busy, demands a lot of attention, pays your bills promptly, and—here's the darker side—causes you more aggravation than you ever could ever have believed would result. Most of this aggravation stems from the fear you will always carry of doing something, or saying something, that displeases the person who has the power to terminate your employment immediately.

Yes, I speak from experience.

Back in the late 1980's, President Ronald Reagan had Congress pass legislation removing all sorts of bank regulations which had previously put in place safeguards against improvident lending practices. The repeal of these regulations led many financial institutions to make all kinds of horribly under-secured, high-risk loans on business and construction projects, many of which failed and, in turn, left many hundreds of millions of dollars of loans "in default". This became known as the "savings and loans crisis". As a young lawyer back then, I was introduced to the general counsel of a midsized North Jersey bank who had file drawers filled with foreclosure cases and lawsuits for monies owed to the bank on their portfolio of these failed loans. This bank had a "short list" of approved law firms to handle such matters, and, because this was not New York City, the firms on the approved list were not gigantic law factories but what might be considered midsize firms in any large city. The bank's general litigation counsel came to know that my firm (at the time, comprised of 14 or so lawyers, and then based in New York City but with a New Jersey office), specialized in construction-related issues, and he concluded that my firm could handle the matters just as competently as some of the larger firms he generally dealt with.

I also took a different approach to the loans in default, explaining to counsel that I believed the bank would be better off not fighting to a judgment (with all the issues that entails including the expense involved as well as whether any judgment obtained could be collected). Instead, we would try re-negotiating the terms of the loan so they would no longer be classified as "in default". Thus, the loan in issue could be placed back into the performing loan category on the bank's books. Such practices came to be known as a "loan workout", whereby terms acceptable to both the bank and the borrower, were reached...hopefully leading to eventual, complete repayment, albeit over a longer period of time. The borrower got a second chance at completing his project, and if the "workout" agreement failed to produce the right result, the bank would take over the collateral without more litigation. So, both borrower and lender had strong incentives to make a deal along these lines.

Landing this client was a coup for me, and for years the bank was more than happy with the services my colleagues and I provided. And it resulted in a lot of reliable, profitable legal work.

But as I've said, when you have a big, marquee client, there won't be a paper you file, or a letter sent on that client's behalf, that won't cause you some level of stress...and more significant actions will bring more significant stress. Bottom line: there will always—*always*—be a lingering fear that the day will come when something goes awry, or maybe the client simply gets taken over in a merger, and that newly merged company will no longer send you or your firm all that work.

For years, I lived with that feeling. And many a night, I would wake up and jump out of bed to make lists, or add to a list I already started. Things like: *"Double-check to see if the Answer on the bank's new matter was served"* ...or, *"Did we send the mortgage in on the _____ matter to be recorded?"* ...or, *"Call Andy about the offer from Ted on the Maine deal"* ...or, *"Send Dave the new draft workout plan"* ...and on and on. I lost a lot of sleep, but yes, I also made a lot of money.

After several years, some mid-level loan bank officer decided he didn't want to work with me or my firm any longer. We had enjoyed a good working relationship right up until that day. But then, the bank's in-house counsel called and asked my firm to send all the bank's open files to another law firm on their approved list. That was it; the relationship was over, and there was just no salvaging it. Every good result that I achieved over the years—all the things, large and small, that the officers and directors (and in-house counsel) were not only happy with, but outright laudatory about—counted for little that day. I never learned whether a real issue had arisen or whether a "problem" was manufactured. It was just that old saying playing out: "*Yeah, but what have you done for us today?*"

Since that time, I have spoken to many small firm practitioners who have lived through the Big Client Experience, and each has described very similar relationships, events, and circumstances.

If you are lucky enough to have such a client, enjoy it as long as it lasts. But remember, all relationships end at some point. As one friend said to me, "*Sure, you had a good case of frayed nerves for years, but it was a great ride financially while it lasted, wasn't it?*" It was.

Having personally lived through this scenario, I can tell you that it's not such a bad thing to have the majority of your business come from many smaller clients as opposed to a few large ones. If you lose one or even several, others can and will replace them over time, and losing any single client is never likely to make you miss a rent or mortgage payment.

7
"I WOULD RATHER PAY YOU THAN PAY HIM"

IF YOUR CLIENT REFUSES TO SETTLE EVEN THE VERY SMALL CLAIM, YOU MAY BE WALKING INTO A QUAGMIRE.

At the outset of any matter, be careful if a client says to you, "*I would rather pay you than pay him*". I can promise you that if your client utters these or similar words, and refuses to settle even a small claim, it's probably going to be a difficult case: Difficult to resolve on reasonable terms, and difficult to collect your fee.

You have no idea how many times you will hear clients say something like, "*Hey, f%$K that guy. I would rather pay you $20,000 than to pay him a dime*". Only later, when the client's emotions cool, he will ask how in heck his legal bills even got to $20,000, although you dutifully sent him monthly statements of everything you were doing, detailing all the services you performed, and all the costs charged by each attorney that worked on the file.

Under such circumstances, I *could* advise you to draft a letter to the client, outlining the situation and your recommendations for settlement, and how you had been directed by him to fight the matter despite your advice. But producing that letter later, showing what your clear advice was at the outset, will only make the client angrier. He will say he does not recall your counsel. And even if he does, he will not like you any better for remembering to put it in writing, and like you still less for making him remember it. In short, this is one of those times when the conflict between running your business and trying to do the best for your client is stark.

In short, there are no winners here.

Even after 35+ years of practice, I have yet to meet any

practitioner who has stumbled upon, or reasoned out, a practical solution to this scenario. I can tell you this: I have walked away from many thousands of dollars in billings to salvage good client relationships when early settlements of these kinds of disputes could not be reached. I have also considered rejecting the case at the outset after carefully explaining to the client why I would rather not be involved. But if the client is one you consider a good, steady client, you never want to give them reason to look for another lawyer. The client may never return if he believes, rightly or wrongly, that you turned your back on him.

The only time I ever actually rejected such a case was with a new client (after explaining why), or with a client I didn't mind losing. And, by the way, I have yet to see any new matters from those I did turn away under such circumstances. So, think it through before you act, and whichever course you choose, *put your advice in writing to the client.*

8

A MATTER OF PRINCIPLE VS. PRINCIPAL, PART 1

THE "TOO-SMALL CASE" IS A KILLER FOR THE ATTORNEY-CLIENT RELATIONSHIP; YOU WILL WORK JUST AS HARD ON THE $20,000 MATTER AS YOU WILL ON THE $220,000 MATTER.

My friend John W is a very practical lawyer who has dealt countless times with the issue I described in the previous essay. It is what he calls the "too-small case".

John says these matters inevitably lead him to discuss with clients the positives and negatives of a lawsuit, and the conversation usually ends with him asking the client, "*How do you spell 'principle?'*" Because while some clients will insist that the case ... "*is a matter of principle*" (translation: *I don't want to let the other guy hold me up for money he doesn't deserve*), the client's *principles* will eventually require him to write a check or checks to you for a whole lot of *principal*, whether to the lawyer, to the adversary, or both.[1]

When it comes to "too-small cases", I have yet to meet a client who likes to hear that paying a few thousand dollars to someone who may, in their mind, not deserve it is still cheaper and less bothersome than fighting. "*You have a business to run*," I'll remind my client, "*And this lawsuit will only be an expensive distraction*".

So, what else can you do you do when a "too-small case" lands in *your* lap?

Your first call should be to your adversary.

The only real hope you have to resolve the matter as

---

[1] Word play by John Walsh, Jr. Esq. (used with permission), who specializes in Trusts and Estates work in Northern New Jersey, New York City, and Florida.

inexpensively as possible is that you get lucky when you reach out to the other lawyer, and actually speak with someone who believes as you do, and who convinces his client to pay or settle...quickly and within reason. What you hope to accomplish is a speedy resolution for a fair amount; what some lawyers refer to as "an annoyance sum" of money.

But let me expound a bit why these problem cases have important ramifications for you as well:

There is no way you can tell a client, "*I will fight this as long as you want to*", and then expect to be paid for all your efforts. I mean, how can you bill a client for, say, $50,000, for the time you actually invested to prosecute, or to defend a case in which $7,000, $10,000, or even $30,000, is the amount in issue? Well, you *can*, but you will not keep that client for very long. On the other hand, sometimes the client has to fight such a case because there are business-related ramifications for *not* doing so. After all, no business can afford to have a reputation that if it is sued, it will automatically pay the other guy "something".

Frankly, the "too-small case" is a killer for the attorney-client relationship because you will work just as hard on the $20,000 matter as you will on the $220,000 matter. In a typical commercial matter, the facts do not differ from one to another all that much.

Here's an example:

If A sues B for a defective motor, the defect may cost $20,000 to remediate. But if A sues B for a defective piece of sophisticated equipment (say a large complex machine like a construction crane), repairing that defect may add $600,000 to the damages. And yet the issues to be tried (sale of a defective piece of equipment that had to be repaired), and the effort and time needed to present the case, will not differ all that much. So, when—not *if*—a similar situation comes your way, you have to decide whether this is a case your client *wants* or *needs* to bring, or *wants* or *needs* to defend? And is it worth getting yourself involved in it? As I have said before, if the matter has been brought to you by a good, steady client, it will be extremely hard (nearly impossible) to reject the case that he or she wants you to handle. You never want to tell a good client they need to find another lawyer to help them (unless the matter is beyond your expertise).

A personal example:

I have long represented a small, family-owned construction contracting business. The firm's founder was a solid citizen; a man of his word, and someone for whom a handshake was as good as any written agreement.

One day, a general construction contractor asked my client's company to perform some construction on the entrance of a small storefront medical office. It was to be part of a much larger renovation project. So, on the promise—and handshake—of the general contractor, my client sent his standard purchase order. The general contractor signed and returned it, and work got underway. In a matter of a few weeks, my client finished his part of the renovation, and he requested to be paid the full contract sum...all of $30,500.

Of course, the general contractor did *not* pay, or I would not have this story to relate.

I explained to my client that if the other side did not see the value in settling early, any suit in a New York Court to collect this money was surely going to cost more in legal fees and costs than the amount he was owed. So, with the goal of maximizing the sum collected and minimizing the costs associated with collecting it, I made a phone call to the general contractor's lawyer. Not only did he not desire to settle, he offered my client *nothing* for the work that was fully performed. Not a cent. After relating to my client the brief, unhappy conversation I had with that attorney, we assumed that the attorney—and maybe his client, too—were hoping that no one in their right mind would sue for $30,500 in New York.

They were wrong.

When the general contractor became convinced that my client was not going to roll over or walk away, he sued my client for $75,000, allegedly for failing to perform the renovation work correctly. We filed a counterclaim for the $30,500 my client was owed, plus interest on bills not paid, plus counsel fees, which my client's Purchase Order's terms allowed.[2] Even had my client not been forced by the filing of a suit, he explained that he had to sue because, as a small contractor, he could not afford to have a reputation that he could be taken advantage of. In other words, he could not allow "the street" to believe that his firm would walk away from money it rightly earned.

Believe it or not, because the other lawyer, and his client would not even discuss settlement (at any time), the case ran on for four years. Every attempt I made to discuss settlement—which occurred at least once every several weeks—was met with a stone-cold reprise: "*We are not settling*". What's more, everything that could be done to wear us down was tried by our adversary. You would have thought millions of dollars were at stake.

Long story short, we won the case.

---

[2] In the United States, most jurisdictions (and New York is among them) do not allow for an award of attorney fees to a winning party unless there is a specific contract clause that provides for it, or an asserted claim is based on a statute that expressly provides for an award of attorney fees.

After four years, the general contractor's bogus claims were dismissed, and we convinced the Court that we were owed every dime we billed. To date, we have collected a grand total of $33,500. This sounds good until you also learn we were awarded a judgment that provided not only for the payment of the claimed principal sum, but also $54,000 in counsel fees, as well as almost $12,000 in interest. To the date of this writing, we have been unable to collect on *any* of these additional sums.

Cases like these, as I said before, can destroy an otherwise great attorney-client relationship. Because no good can ever come from the case where the sum in dispute is dwarfed by even the most conservative estimates of the lawyers' fees and other costs involved to bring such a matter to Court.[3]

In this case, however, while I could never expect to collect all of the fees I billed, I was fortunate.

I sat down with my client, and I agreed to slice and dice my bill until he was comfortable. And because he was a good client for whom I had genuine respect, my solution to accept far less money for the case than was billed and earned was the only practical solution. Even though it took four years to resolve, my client felt his case was completely vindicated. And any contractor or customer of his who tries to play the "same game" quickly learns about what is now a matter of public record; that he will never just lie down if wronged.

So, what did I get out of this fiasco? Well, for one thing, I maintained, and built upon, a good client relationship. That client knows he has an attorney who is truly on his side. The respect and

---

[3] The one exception to this rule is where you win the case with an award of attorney fees, and you actually collect it all from the adversary. In that instance, it's a fight for who (lawyer or client) will pay the celebratory bar bill.

trust between my firm and this client has even led to a friendship, and every once in a while my phone rings from someone who says, "*David at ABC Glass told me to call you*".

9

A MATTER OF PRINCIPLE VS. PRINCIPAL, PART 2

IF YOU DEVELOP A RAPPORT WITH YOUR CLIENT, YOU MAY WANT TO HOLD ONTO THE CASE EVEN IF IT'S LIKELY TO BE A LOSS-LEADER.

Let's look at how else to address the "too-small case."

Some attorneys refer their own client to other lawyers who specialize in "collections". These lawyers usually work on a contingency fee arrangement and take between a 25%-40% piece of what is recovered in a commercial matter. But there are two good reasons why you might want to think twice before you ever refer a client to another attorney for "cost" reasons.

First, you may well be setting your client up for a very frustrating experience because collection lawyers tend to like simple collection matters. You know the type: A sells goods to B, and B doesn't pay A all he was owed. But, in construction, commercial, or other more complex matters, any claim for the money owed is almost always met with counterclaims that have to be defended. Collection lawyers either shy away from such matters altogether, or if they do take the case and defend the counterclaim, they often want to charge by the hour for the defense work. Or, worse, and especially if they don't charge for those services, they often fail to adequately prepare to understand the counterclaim. The result? The case is often lost, resolved on very low payouts, or even in what attorneys call "walk-away" deals. These are settlements where both attorneys generally recognize that they will put in far too much time to approach the case economically or properly, so they convince their respective clients to just agree to *walk away*. If you are the party who legitimately owes the other party money, that is a good deal. If you are a merchant or provider of services who never got paid by his customer, that's a deal you would rather do without.

A second good reason for *not* sending your client to another lawyer is obvious:

Once you refer a client down the street, it is a possibility that you may never see that client again. Why? Well, it may be because the client went to an attorney who tried to talk him into "walking away", and he is not happy that you sent him there. But it also may turn out that the attorney you referred the matter to may prove to be as equally skilled as you are, more personable, have a nicer office, or charge less ... or any combination of such variables.

So, what's the take-away here?

If you like the client, and are developing a rapport with him, maybe this is one case you stick with the client on ... even if it is a possible loss-leader. The client will more than appreciate your standing up for him, especially if you, like me, end up taking it on the chin yourself. I know that in the short term it's not great for business. But long term, it may lead to the best advertising for your services there ever was or will be: Another satisfied client that refers business. No attorney I know ever gets tired of receiving a phone call from someone you never heard of who begins the conversation with, *"You don't know me, but David Smith told me to call you because I have a problem, and he told me how you helped him out"*.

Section IV
BUILDING A GOOD REPUTATION HELPS BUILD YOUR PRACTICE

1
WHEN THE CLIENT CALLS...ANSWER

TOO MANY LAWYERS BELIEVE THEIR INVOICES ARE ALL THAT A LAW FIRM NEEDS FOR CLIENT COMMUNICATION.

If I can make just one thing clear in this book, let it be this: Communicate often and clearly with your clients. In fact, Rule #1 in every law office should be: *"Promptly respond to your client emails and return their phone calls".*

Too many lawyers believe their invoices are all that a law firm needs for client communication. After all, they reason, most billing software generates bills that provide a lot of vital information; the services performed, the date of those services, and they identify which lawyers rendered what services.

Call this "communication" if you like...but it's not nearly enough.

In fact, it is absolutely stunning how many times I have heard from clients, or even other attorneys' clients, the following complaint...or something very close to it: *"My last lawyer was impossible to contact. He never returned my calls. I never knew where things stood on my case."* Can you imagine letting a paying client go because you didn't have the five or ten minutes it takes to call him/her back (even within a day or two) after they take the time to call you and leave a message? And, can you imagine allowing a disgruntled client to spread this kind of information about you? There is no excuse for this lapse, especially when you can dash off an email in minutes, or leave a voice message for someone even after your work day is otherwise over. It's so easy, and it pays dividends in ways you will never be able to calculate.

When a client entrusts a matter to you or your firm, they actually have earned the right to ask about it from time to time. Wouldn't you want to know if anything of interest was taking place on your case if it was a matter of importance to you? But if you practice what I preach—frequent and open communication with clients—the number of calls you will have to return will actually diminish over time because the need to contact *you* falls if it is you *who* contacts the client. Your clients will come to understand that if there is something to report, you will call or write to them.

But there is another added benefit...potential new clients.

If I hear people complaining about lawyers not returning phone calls, how many other people out there, their friends and co-workers, are hearing the same thing? You never know, but one person complaining about his or her lawyer just might be complaining to one of your clients. How nice it would be to have your client say something like, "*My attorney never ignores my calls. In fact, I usually don't have to call him at all because he lets me know when things happen*". The lesson here? Only good can come from keeping in touch with your clients.

2
BE KNOWN AS A PRACTICAL PRACTITIONER

OVER TIME, YOU WILL GO FURTHER BY BEING THE LAWYER WHO IS KNOWN AS A DEAL-MAKER NOT A DEAL-BREAKER.

When I left the prosecutor's office for civil law, I joined a small New York City construction law boutique firm. It had a solid reputation for handling complex litigation and generally obtaining favorable results for its clients. The firm was founded and essentially owned by three lawyers, each of whom was a very smart and diligent practitioner. Still, their approaches to running the firm (i.e., running the business) was as different as different could be.

Partner #1 always had his eye on profitability. Looking at a new case, he would mentally size up the value in taking on a new matter, quantifying the hours that could be billed. Not to the exclusion of the client's needs, but as a corollary to it.

Partner #2 (one of the best trial lawyers I have ever known) took a different approach. He always put the client first, believing—as I argue in this book—that doing right by the client will benefit the "business" side of the firm in the long run.

Partner #3 generally left running the "business" to the other two, and he concentrated on being the best advocate he could be.

One day, one of the firm's clients came in to discuss a large claim he wished to pursue against the City of New York, arising out of a very large, expensive, multi-year municipal construction project. The claim was valued in the millions of dollars. At that time, the City of New York employed over 100 attorneys in its Corporation Counsel's office, and, for the most part, these lawyers were very skilled at what they did. As a result, most cases filed against the City were strenuously defended.

Partner #1 saw this particular client's case as one that would generate hundreds if not thousands of billable hours over a period of years. And, if normal procedure were followed, that is exactly what would have occurred because the matter was very complex, and it would have involved a careful review of literally thousands of documents to begin the process of litigation.

But Partner #2, who possessed an incredible ability to spot the critical issues in any case merely by reviewing the file, noticed early on that the dispute mainly centered on the parties' differing interpretations of a *single* part of the contract that governed this massive construction project. He also noticed that the person most directly responsible for the project for the City was someone he had known a long time and had litigated against for many years. Within several days (not weeks or months), Partner #2 had called the City's law department to explain why he thought litigating this claim for years would be detrimental to both our client and the City.

What followed was a series of phone calls in which he ultimately convinced the City's representatives to set up a meeting so the client's claim could be reviewed and discussed with City lawyers and construction engineers. Ordinarily, this process back then took place only after many years of litigation in court after the matters in issue could be identified.

But because Partner #2 was able to convince the City that the issues to be discussed were already identifiable and sufficiently "narrow", the parties began a long series of discussions and negotiations at which every aspect of the client's claim was reviewed, discussed, and vetted in a businesslike way. In a comparatively short amount of time, Partner #2 had convinced his adversaries that doing *what was right* (in this instance, avoiding a multi-year court battle and paying the contractor-client an awful lot more money because it was in fact owed it under the terms of its contract) was the course they should follow. The other option open to the City was to insist on non-payment just because they could, and thereby cause a long, drawn-out litigation.

A few years after these events, I met with an extremely experienced lawyer for coffee, and asked his opinion about how that case was handled. What he told me, I remember to this day: "*Many lawyers would not agree with me, but I believe over time you get further by being the lawyer who is known as a deal-maker not a deal-breaker.*" Ever since that day, I have tried to be a deal-*maker*, reaching settlements that greatly benefited the client and, in the process, raised the reputation of my firm even though it might have meant many fewer billable hours.

Which brings to mind an oft-told lawyer joke:

It's about an old lawyer who had one very large and significant estate matter for a wealthy—but deceased—client named Bond. Well, the matter had been open so long it was simply referred to in the courts and among lawyers involved as, "The Bond Estate Case". As the joke goes, this old lawyer was using the Bond estate as his law firm's personal annuity, billing time on it as often as possible over the course of many years. One day, the old lawyer brought his son, a new lawyer, into the practice, and then went on vacation. Upon returning home, the old lawyer asked his son for a report, and the young man said, "*Dad, dad, you're going to be so proud of me, I settled the Bond estate*"! To which his father, clutching his chest, replies, "*YOU DID WHAT??*"

My advice to you: Put your client and his needs first.

There will be many cases that cry out for an insightful lawyer who is able to discern what a dispute is really about, and who can suggest a sensible, workable, acceptable resolution very early in the process. Not every case fits the bill. Indeed, to find a workable, early but satisfactory solution to a dispute requires that the other party's lawyer (or parties' lawyers) see matters the way you do. But do yourself and your clients a lasting favor: Be known as a practical practitioner.

3

THE HUMAN ELEMENT OF BEING A LAWYER AND ADVOCATE

IT IS NOT A SIGN OF WEAKNESS OR FRIVOLITY TO ACT LIKE A REAL HUMAN. BEING OPEN AND PERSONABLE WON'T UNDERMINE THE "SERIOUSNESS" OF YOUR POSITION.

I know many good lawyers who are possessed of personalities that are, shall I say, extremely dry. They will take on a matter and stick to the facts as they see them, but who also take on a persona that is more like an emotionless machine than a person. These lawyers are sometimes difficult to deal with, as they seem to completely lack all desire to engage in a personal conversation of any kind as they plod inexorably forward "by the book". In short, there is simply no personal rapport in any of their lawyer-to-lawyer discussions or phone calls. They take their business, and themselves, *very* seriously. One might also say that they have absolutely no sense of humor.

I believe this attitude takes the human element out of professional communications, and often makes any effort at settling cases more difficult. I am not sure why this is so because I am always amazed how many cases ultimately get resolved between lawyers when the germ of the idea is mentioned during genuinely friendly lawyer-to-lawyer conversations. There is nothing about being open and personable in any way that undermines, or is inconsistent with, producing quality pleadings and briefs, or the aggressive representation of your clients' interests. Why more lawyers are not willing to engage in even the briefest repartee is a mystery to me. I suppose they believe it undermines the seriousness of their position, or something like that.

When my office hires professionals, we look for personable, quality attorneys who take their jobs, but not themselves, very seriously. We want to work with people we actually enjoy being around. After all, one's *work* life is a large part of one's life. I think that unless you have a reason to go through life acting like an android, it is not a sign of weakness, or frivolity, to act like a real human.

4
ON REPUTATION, PART 1

A GOOD REPUTATION IS THE ONE THING THAT HAS THE GREATEST VALUE TO ANY PRACTICING LAWYER.

Establishing trust, not just with those whom you work, but with your *adversaries*, too, is invaluable.

Personal story:

About six years ago, a professional engineer called me on a referral. He had a contract dispute with an architect who hired him to work on some building plans for a public works project. The engineer was owed some $200,000, and he said he wanted to sue the architect "immediately" having heard the architect's firm was "in trouble".

As it turned out, the firm had fallen on lean times, and had already filed for protection under the United States Bankruptcy Code. (Note: as a general aside, fighting a bankrupt entity is not a winning proposition. Bankruptcy Courts are too often overly lenient with debtors, and it is very hard to win a suit against a bankrupt party. What's worse, even if you "win", you only end up with a claim in the Bankruptcy process, and it will reap only so much as the bankrupt party's estate can pay, which is usually a small percentage—if anything—on every dollar of your claim. However, in New York, where this claim was pending, monies earned on a construction project are, by statute, "trust funds" and are not considered the bankrupt party's money. As a result, if you prove your claim, you are generally entitled to be paid all of the money you are owed.)

I explained all this in detail to my client, who desired to press ahead.

After investigating the matter, I came to learn that I knew several of the key lawyers in the pending Bankruptcy proceedings, including the architect's lawyer, the creditors' committee's lawyer, and a couple of large creditors' counsel. In a matter of weeks—not months or years—and merely by phoning the lawyers I knew and asking what could be done for my creditor-client, I was able to cut through much of the usual Bankruptcy red tape. My client's claim was re-categorized by the bankrupt architect from "disputed" to "un-disputed", and, in what proved to be surprisingly short order, my firm received a check for almost the full sum sought.

No lawsuit was filed, no invectives exchanged. And all because the major players in the proceedings knew me, trusted me, and knew that when I said we could—and *would* prove the claim—through an adversary proceeding if need be (meaning a lawsuit within the context of the bankruptcy proceedings), they understood I would do just that. What made this all work so smoothly is that even though I did not have personal relationship with all of the major players, those lawyers had relationships with the ones I *did* know, and they trusted them! It helped to have a reputation for trustworthiness.

I believe a good reputation is the one thing that has the greatest value to any practicing lawyer.

As your career develops, you want Judges and other lawyers to know you (and if they do not know you, to know someone who does), who can say about you, "*He is a good lawyer, a stand-up guy (or gal), and a straight-shooter*". Tricks, deception, deceit, and sleight of hand may make for dramatic treatment in the movies and on TV. But in real life, those qualities can only tarnish your reputation, and if *that* is your reputation, no one will ever know when to trust you, or the client you represent.

5
ON REPUTATION, PART 2

IN THE LONG RUN, HAVING A REPUTATION FOR TRUST AND HONESTY CAN MAKE A DIFFERENCE WITH ADVERSARIES AND JUDGES.

About 14 years ago, I became involved in a multi-party case pending in the U.S. District Court for the Eastern District of New York. There were four separate parties represented by counsel. The matter had been referred by the District Judge to a Magistrate to address and rule on all matters relating to discovery in the case. We'd already been to several conferences and were preparing the case for a possible summary judgment motion, or failing that, trial.

One day, while at another lawyer's office on a wholly different matter, my office reached me by phone to advise that a conference was taking place before the Magistrate and that all parties were there at that very moment *waiting for me*. I checked my diary (calendar) and saw nothing about a conference scheduled for that day. Somehow, I had forgotten to write it into my appointment schedule, and this particular Magistrate was one tough "no-nonsense" Judge. I immediately called his courtroom and explained that "I blew it"; no excuses. I apologized profusely, not just to the Magistrate but also to all counsel in attendance. I said that if, given 30 or 40 minutes, I would leave the meeting I was in immediately, pick up my file and hustle myself down to the Magistrate's courtroom.

At that point two things happened:

First, I heard in the background a discussion among all counsel and then one clear voice said something like, *"Judge, we* all have dealt with Mr. Lesser on this matter for months. He would not skip a conference on this case intentionally; mistakes happen to all of us". Imagine my surprise. In the face of a chance to kick an adversary when he is down (or at least, for the moment, held in disfavor by the Court) they let it pass.

The Magistrate, though clearly not happy, paused and said, "Mr. Lesser, you have appeared before me, correct?"

Yes, I said.

At this point, I felt surely I was about to be lectured with a "then-you-know-my rules" admonition!

Instead, the Magistrate must have recalled something positive about that past interaction, as he said, *"Mr. Lesser, there is no need at this point for you to run back to your office now. I will allow you to appear by phone today"*. I was completely taken aback; I had never seen this Magistrate ever cut a break to any attorney who failed to follow his well-established rules.

There is no question in my mind that had I not developed the rapport of trust and honesty with those attorneys sitting in front of him, that this Magistrate would have made what was already an unpleasant situation, many, many times worse. As it turned out, that case went on for many months and never once did the Magistrate mention the incident to me (or hold it against me). Chalk this one up as another example of what a good reputation can do for you.

I also want to take this opportunity to mention the conduct of my adversaries in this case.

If you are the attorney in the courtroom at the appointed time when your adversary is absent, it would be so easy to take advantage of that fact. Whether verbally, or simply with a shared "eyeroll", one could convey to the Judge something along the lines of, *"I'm here as required. But this other attorney is so unreliable; a real piece of work*". Don't be that kind of adversary. Either say nothing at all or stand up for your adversary if he or she is worth it. It will only burnish your image of propriety and professionalism with the Court. And don't forget to read (*in Section VI*) about the importance of attending conferences.

6

THE "BLACK SHOE" LAWYER

IF YOU'VE GOT A REPUTATION FOR BEING AN OPEN, ACCESSIBLE LAWYER WILLING TO SPEAK WITH ADVERSARIES, TAKING THE "MAD DOG" APPROACH WILL ADVERSELY IMPACT YOUR IMAGE.

You've probably heard the phrase "white shoe lawyer". It refers to the genteel, high-end, highly educated lawyer who enjoys a magnificent office as part of a large, mostly white male old-line law firm representing large, deep-pocketed corporations and/or wealthy families. The image is generally one of a person who does not get his hands (or his shoes) dirty.

On the other hand, I once knew a litigator in a large firm who, with more than just a bit of a mischievous glint in his eye, proudly referred to himself as a "black shoe lawyer". By this, he meant that he was the sort of lawyer who took no prisoners, and who litigated every case extremely aggressively. No gentlemanly stuff for him, and he was fortunate that he had well-heeled clients who paid his large bills for his very aggressive, labor-intensive lawyering. He, and the attorneys he supervised, billed hundreds of hours on almost every matter, large and small. He was proud of the fact, and made it well known that he loved to outspend any opponent, and "bury" them in litigation, believing in that form of "justice". He actually wanted this to be his reputation, and it was.

Sometimes this is exactly the kind of lawyering that is called for in a given matter, and it might help develop your practice, or niche, if you can be that kind of person *when the circumstances warrant it.*

But be careful.

I, for one, do not believe that you can be both the kind of

attorney who is known as a straight-shooting practical practitioner, who looks to resolve disputes rather than continue them, and also be the "black shoe" practitioner. If that is what your client really wants, maybe you have to assign someone else in your own office, or refer the client to another firm. This is especially true if in your assessment of the matter at hand, that kind of lawyering will not help (or might even hurt) your client's cause. If you've been honing a reputation for being an open, accessible lawyer willing to speak with adversaries, taking the "mad dog" approach—even in other, limited circumstances—will adversely impact your image.

Section V
RETAINERS AND BILLING THAT WORK FOR YOU

1
THE IMPORTANCE OF CLEAR RETAINERS

THE CONTENT OF YOUR RETAINER IS IMPORTANT FOR A NUMBER OF REASONS.

Okay, so you decide to take on a new client.

Many jurisdictions now require that you have a signed retainer for each new client (and some jurisdictions may even require new retainers for each new matter). As always, check the rules.

The content of your retainer is important for a number of reasons.

First, if you are taking on a case for a corporate client, and you are unsure of the company's ability to pay, you will likely want the principal's personal guarantee of payment. In most jurisdictions a guarantee must be clear and must be in writing.

Second, you should clearly specify the hourly rate or other payment terms agreed upon. I suggest that the retainer also include the time within which you expect payment to be made. In fact, my firm's form retainer states that the client has agreed to pay the firm's bills within 10 days of receipt unless the client disputes any aspect of the invoice, in which case the client must place his objections to any aspect of the charges he receives in writing, and that payment be remitted for any undisputed portion of the bill. Such a clause will help you collect what you are owed if the client "gets behind" in payments (as so many do), and then tries to argue that he did not pay because he had issues with the services rendered or the billing.

Some firms require that the client maintain a certain balance in escrow with the firm at all times. This is a great practice if you have the kind of clients who can afford to undertake, and live up to, that obligation. But if you are like most practitioners in solo and small-to-medium sized firms, you may be reading this suggestion and thinking, "*Yeah, I wish*".

In some fields of practice, the client virtually dictates all of the aspects of the terms of the retainer and the manner in which billing must be submitted. This most often occurs when representing insurance companies. But other large corporate clients often lay down the procedures that must be followed for a bill to be processed for payment. There is very little room to negotiate these terms and the best one can usually hope for is to get an agreement on an upward departure from the typically low hourly rates such a client wants to pay. This is not always easy or even possible as these firms hold a lot of sway, following the Golden Rule. You know, that's the one that says, "*He who has the gold makes the rules*". Their operating theory is, "*If you don't want our work, there are lines of lawyers behind you that do*". Unfortunately, they're right.

2

DIFFICULTIES WITH CONTINGENCY CASE RETAINERS

DON'T TAKE EVERY CASE THAT WALKS IN THE DOOR, EVEN IF A DESIRABLE CLIENT INSISTS ON A CONTINGENCY FEE ARRANGEMENT.

Contingency cases only pay a fee when settled; or, if tried, when the judgment is collected.[4]

Unless you have a different source of operating funds, signing up all—or most of your clients—to straight contingency cases should be avoided if you are just starting on your own or with others in a small firm, as these cases usually require many hours of work without any cash flow.

Sure, there are some matters taken on a contingency that are settled very easily, and these provide a bit of a windfall in that the amount of work you thought would be required to reach the point of settlement or judgment took but a fraction of that. But you cannot bank on that. So, sometimes you just have to say "no", and not take every case that walks in the door, even if a desirable client is insisting on a pure contingency fee arrangement.

One particular problem with contingency cases is that too many lawyers get trapped by having an overly optimistic, or greedy, client who refuses to accept what any objective person would say is a fair—or even excellent—settlement. The client's

---

[4] Former Dean John J. Murphy of St. John's Law School in New York comically instructed his students on how to explain to a client how a contingency case works. "Explain it this way," he said. "If we lose the case, I get *nothing*. But if we win the case, *you* get nothing".

reasoning goes something like this: *"I was offered this amount now. I am not paying anything to have my lawyer keep working the case, so I will reject this and press the case forward, hopefully getting a higher offer later"*.

You may desire to resign from a case at this point. And if you and your client do have a parting of the ways, most, if not all, of the States will recognize that you have a lien on any proceeds the case may produce (if any) for the work you have put in to that point. That does not mean you *have* to exit the case if the client turns down the offer. You may have re-assessed the matter as the case moved along and want to see it through to the end. In fact, lawyers and clients are constantly re-assessing their cases, as well they should, as discovery proceeds and sheds new light on the "facts" you thought existed. Of course, if you resign a case, or are discharged by the client, the next lawyer has to successfully try the case or settle it for you to collect any fee.

No one ever wrote a law that prevented a lawyer from getting creative with retainer agreements, *provided* they meet the governing State's ethical requirements, are fair, and have been well-explained to the client.

My suggestion is that if you are going to take on a matter on a straight contingency basis that you first have a conversation with the client as to what a fair expectation of the real value of the case is. Build the amount into your retainer agreement (with any appropriate adjustments as the case moves forward) stating that, if you get a settlement offer at or above that level, the client will either accept it or allow you to be relieved from the case at that juncture.

If a settlement that you deem to be fair is refused by the client, then absent an agreed-upon exit strategy being built into the retainer agreement, you will now be forced to continue to work on the case...even take the case to trial on your dime.[5] That means you will have to devote more valuable time to the case to prepare for trial and try the case, and, further, to invest more expenses for experts and the like. All of that extra work and expense when your agreed client's goal (the settlement amount) was already achieved by your efforts. The trap is further damaging because if you received the fair settlement offer, it is likely that your adversary believed the offer to be fair as well. Absent new, compelling information, the offer is not likely to be materially increased before trial.

I know one lawyer with whom I discussed this subject who said she had this exact problem once. Her solution was to approach the judge and explain the situation, and then ask the Court's assistance in getting the client to see reason. But even if that solution is viable on some occasions, it won't be available or practical in many others. Not every judge is going to spend time trying to convince your client to accept a settlement. This is why knowing the kind of client you have allowed to retain you is vitally important.

---

[5] I stress the importance of checking your particular jurisdiction's practice rules before drafting any retainer. While I can think of many reasons not to allow it, it may even be permissible in your jurisdiction to draft a retainer agreement that requires the client to accept the sum if offered if you clearly agree to that with the client in advance.

3
SOME CAUTIONS ON CONTINGENCY CASE RETAINERS

CONTINGENCY FEE RETAINERS ARE GENERALLY GOVERNED BY THE LOCAL RULES OF PRACTICE AND ETHICAL CONSIDERATIONS; CHECK YOUR LOCAL RULES BEFORE DRAFTING THE RETAINER.

Retainers for contingency matters can cause all kinds of problems for lawyers. But if you have an active practice, and can afford the start-up costs of funding contingency cases, the settlements can prove very lucrative. In addition, collection issues are often minimized by the fact that many such matters are accident cases defended by insurance companies who pay when they settle or lose.

If you are drafting a contingency retainer, be mindful that contingency fee retainers are generally governed by the local rules of practice and ethical considerations. Check your local rules *before* you draft your contingency (or other) retainers. You do not want to run afoul of ethics rules; violations of rules governing retainers and fees may impair your ability to collect any fee at all. But some problems may be avoidable, or at least minimized, by a clearly worded retainer agreement.

Case books are filled with examples of lawyers who took on a contingency case, and, for one reason or another, never finished the case and another lawyer took their place. Then, when the case finally settles, or a favorable judgment is rendered, the first lawyer seeks to be paid for his services, and invariably there's a fight over how much—or how little—he should receive. If you are taking on a contingency matter, write into your retainer agreement what the client will agree in advance is a fair hourly fee, or a fair percentage, for your efforts, linking your agreed-in-advance fees to each stage of the proceedings. So, for example, you might provide that you will be paid at the rate of $275/hour for work up to the start of discovery; so much per hour for in court time, etc.

You should also provide that if you withdraw, or are relieved as counsel, you can show the retainer to any new lawyer(s) who might come into the case and direct them to pay you from the settlement proceeds, if any. While there might be additional issues you need to address (and no one can think of all of them in advance), a lawyer shown such an agreement will likely thank you for alerting them to an issue that the client failed to mention. He or she will likely not ignore your claim, and at least would agree to escrow your claimed "fee", or allow you time to make an application to the court to protect the portion of the proceeds you claim until the matter is resolved.

4
BILLINGS: MAKE THEM DETAILED AND CLEAR

USE YOUR BILLS TO KEEP THE CLIENT INFORMED AS TO WHAT THEY ARE PAYING FOR; SHOW THEM THAT SOMETHING IS BEING ACCOMPLISHED.

If you are like most general practitioners, you bill for your services by the hour. And if so, there are many easily installed software programs that will automatically generate bills for the work you do and, if you choose, to keep records of payments, disbursements, and profitability, among other things. A good timekeeping program allows you to detail the services you rendered on any given day, and advises the client of other factors, including the name of the attorney, paralegal or clerk who performed the services; the amount of time spent by each in the performance of those services; and the date on which the services were rendered.

Most lawyers hate to do billing. It is a task that, perhaps ironically, you cannot bill for, and yet it takes time to describe the services you have rendered. However, if you do bill by the hour, it is wise to be as detailed as you can be in the description of the services you have rendered. Clients appreciate an entry that reads, *"Called attorney for the defendant Smith to discuss issues regarding documents to be produced by him"*, as opposed to one that simply reads, *"telephone call with counsel"*.

Get into a habit of entering your time every day (or at least, every second day). Playing "catch-up" with billing is difficult and even more time-consuming.

While a habit of typing out detailed entries cannot supplant all client communication, it serves to supplement the "frequent and open communication" with clients that I believe fosters better client relationships. It also provides the client with an opportunity to review your services in detail. Clients will more readily pay for services that show their cause is being advanced, as opposed to some vague listing of activities like "call with attorney for Smith" or, "reviewed file and wrote letter". Show that you are doing a task where something is being accomplished. In other words, this is an opportunity to tell the client what he/she is paying for on a monthly basis. *And, there is no excuse for not sending monthly bills while services are in fact being rendered.* It is different if there is a lull in the file and nothing is actually being worked on. But I believe, even then, you should communicate *something* to the client about what is *not* going on and why.

When my firm is retained on any given matter, we tie our retainer letters into our billing practice, by providing notice to the clients that they will receive detailed bills from the firm, and that it is their job to carefully review the bills when received. We ask that bills be reviewed and processed within 10 days, and we advise the client that if they have any issue with any bill (or any portion of it) to put their objection or question in writing. This practice will help if somewhere down the line you (like many attorneys) have a problem getting paid. If the client disputes the bills later, he or she will have a very hard time explaining to a court or arbitrator why no issue was raised earlier as the client agreed to do in the signed retainer agreement. If you do have a dispute about your bills, the client's belated objections will appear to be afterthoughts, and not real.

If, however, your firm mainly bases its services on contingency billing, or on some other method—say, a flat fee—you should still provide monthly statements. A short memo to the client that describes what has transpired or has been accomplished in the past 30 days—whether by email or letter—should be sent to the client on all active matter(s). If you do this as a matter of course, *you* will have a much happier client (i.e., one who doesn't have to call you to find out where matters stand). In sum, use your bills to keep the client informed as to what they are paying for.

5

BILLING: PAY ATTENTION TO WHAT YOUR CLIENT IS BILLED

CLIENTS TEND TO NITPICK LESS IF THEY KNOW YOU ARE TREATING THEM FAIRLY AND HONESTLY, AND THAT YOU HAVE THEIR INTERESTS AND THEIR POCKETBOOK IN MIND.

You enhance your firm's reputation for honesty and fairness if you avoid the appearance of "nickel-and-dime'ing" your clients. What I mean, is that you foster good will if you do not charge for every phone call you make or take part in, or for every piece of mail or email that you read on the client's case.

However, it's a good practice to subtly remind your clients on occasion how many times they spoke to you, or how many times you did something for them but did not charge for it. This is easily accomplished by recording your time as if you had billed for it (that is, recording what activities were undertaken but having the bill read "no charge"). Almost every billing program allows you to do this. This practice also helps avoid arguments with clients over such things as why some other work you undertook for them took longer than they desired.

Clients tend to nitpick less if they know you are treating them fairly and honestly, and entries that read "no charge" convey that you have both their interests and their pocketbook in mind. Sure, if you send a package by overnight carrier, or if you used an outside copy shop to duplicate many hundreds of pages of documents, you can and should bill the client for such disbursements. But your bills should "tie in" the disbursements to the services performed. So, if you did send an overnight package, one of your time entries should refer to what it was you were doing and that you sent something by such a carrier. A little attention to what you are billing can go a long way to fostering even better client relations.

6
TO BILL, OR NOT TO BILL, OFFICE OVERHEAD CHARGES

OVERHEAD CHARGES OPEN TO THE DOOR TO THE NITPICKY ARGUMENTS WITH CLIENTS THAT EVERY LAWYER SHOULD WANT TO AVOID.

In my firm, we not only send detailed monthly bills, we also advise clients up-front that we do not bill for minor in-house copy charges, phone charges, or for typical US mail charges for simple letters. Of course, we do charge for the attorney time engaged in drafting the correspondence, and for taking part in phone calls of significance.

I know that many firms add a "service" or "administrative" fee to every client's bill to cover the cost of having telephones, postage, and making in-house copies. Whatever you call it, this added "fee" typically ranges between 1% and 2% of that month's total bill to the client, and it is added to the bill as a disbursement. The reasoning behind this practice goes something like this: *"We have copiers we pay for; we have a telephone system; we have secretaries; we have postage costs. It adds up to thousands of dollars a year, and we cannot absorb all of that. So, why not bill clients for them?"*

I really cannot think of a great reason *not* to bill these costs. But when we pitch a new client, we are able to look a client squarely in the eye and explain that we realize retaining and paying a lawyer is expensive, so we do not charge for these things as *we consider them part of the cost of our business operations.* We want clients to know that we will try to do everything we can to manage their matter as effectively and as cost-efficiently as we can. Besides, while the practice of billing a percentage of your overhead to all clients may well be a fair way to divide these costs among the clients, it is by no means an accurate method. A client could have a $10,000 bill in one month with minimal mail and copying costs, or none of either.

The only exact method of passing on these kinds of charges would be to keep track of the hundreds, if not thousands, of every charge for every stamp, every copy, every call etc., each and every month. For most firms, that is just too labor-intensive, and takes too much administrative time. It also opens to the door to the nitpicky arguments with clients that every lawyer should want to avoid. You never want to be perceived as part of your client's problems if you can help it.

7
THE IMPORTANCE OF A NON-ENGAGEMENT LETTER

MANY PEOPLE ALLEGE THAT THEY WERE LED TO BELIEVE BY THE ATTORNEY THAT THEIR MATTER WOULD BE HANDLED; IT IS AN AVOIDABLE CAN OF WORMS, AND A NON-ENGAGEMENT LETTER CAN HELP IMMENSELY.

When you decide not to take a case, or accept the representation of a particular client, it is important to protect yourself by sending that person a letter that clearly states that your firm has not accepted the matter. Many lawyers refer to this document as a "non-engagement letter" or a "rejection letter".

Why send a letter to someone you decided *not* to represent? Because it prevents the non-client from claiming, or at least makes it a heck of a lot harder for him to claim, that he left your office with assurances that all would be handled well. Sadly, many people have made allegations against lawyers that they were led to believe by the attorney that their matter would be handled. This allegation is usually made after the time has tolled to file a claim or cause of action, or *after* the time to answer a complaint has passed. It is an avoidable can of worms, and the non-engagement letter can help immensely.

One more word of advice on this important subject: Always send such a letter very soon after the potential client was told *"thanks but no thanks"*. In it, refer to the date that the potential client came to your office, and the date he or she first (and, if appropriate, last) consulted with you. If limitations periods do come into play on the potential client's claim, the reference to dates will help establish that he came in too late, or, conversely, still had time to do whatever it is the non-client had to do. Do not bother to give any opinion as to the validity of the claim or defense. Such information cannot help you later. Simply state that the matter is not a good fit for the firm, that you will not be taking any action on behalf of the person whatsoever, and that you are returning all papers to the rejected client that may have been left with the firm.

You might want to add that another lawyer might see the matter quite differently and advise the client to seek another lawyer. If time may be a problem, a reminder that you advised the client to see another attorney with haste, may also be appropriate. But in these non-engagement letters, "less is more" is a good rule to follow.

Section VI
PRACTICAL ADVICE ON PRACTICING LAW

1
THE SECRET TO EFFECTIVE ADVOCACY

UNPREPARED LAWYERS CAN DO GREAT HARM TO THEIR CLIENTS IN DEPOSITIONS, MEETINGS, NEGOTIATIONS, AND IN ALL OTHER MATTERS OF IMPORTANCE.

When I first started out in law, a truly great trial lawyer advised me to expect to prepare two or more hours *out of court* for every hour spent *in* court because if you are the lawyer who is prepared, you will know the facts of the matter, and you will have a "road map" for the evidence and the process necessary to reach your end goal.

Facing an ill-prepared lawyer as your adversary is a huge gift to you and your client. You can see what I mean if you ever get a chance to see that classic film comedy, *"Where's Poppa?"* In the movie, actor George Segal plays a New York lawyer. In one scene, he arrives late to court, disheveled with an overflowing briefcase. And from the looks of the Judge, his adversaries and the jurors, it's clear he has kept everyone waiting a long time. On the witness stand, a nice, neat-looking older woman is also waiting. As the Judge prods the late-arriving lawyer to get started, you can see him struggling to recall what stage the case has reached, and even what his role is in the trial. Suddenly, Mr. Segal's character launches into a withering cross-examination of the witness. But the more he goes on the attack, the more he empathizes with the witness, who seems honest and totally credible. As he completes his "cross examination", he says something like, "... *and you were fired for that? Why, that's terrible.*" The witness looks straight at him and responds, "*Yes, I know. That's why I hired you!*"

It's a delightful movie...and a cautionary tale.

Stories of unprepared lawyers are abundant in courtrooms all over the country. And each of these stories usually ends badly for the unprepared lawyer, because nothing irritates a Judge—or a jury—more than waiting for the lawyer to appear; or waiting for the lawyer to sort through a stack of papers for his next document; or waiting for the lawyer as he struggles to ask the right question. Unprepared lawyers don't just invoke the ire of participants at a trial, they also do great harm to their clients in depositions, meetings, negotiations, and in all other matters of importance. In fact, the only ones downright gleeful about an unprepared lawyer is the lawyer's adversary, and of course, the adversary's client. Their job has been made so much easier by the other side's incompetence.

I have personally witnessed many scenarios like the one depicted in the movie. And, if truth be known, I have also lived through situations where I knew that my own case had a serious weakness which, if discovered, could be severely detrimental to my client's case. In fact, I have sometimes actually waited for my adversary to wake up and blow a large hole through my case by asking the question that he has never asked; or by reaching out to some damaging witness that I know is out there, and who is presentable, credible, and just begging to be tapped. Somehow, at least so far, that potential bombshell—the proverbial "shoe"—has yet to drop.

The frequency with which this sort of conduct occurs is testament to the multitude of unprepared lawyers that you will undoubtedly meet during your career. While you may lose sleep worrying about the "what if's", the good news is that you, the prepared lawyer, will have known all along what the other side never discovered, and, if it ever is discovered, at least you will be prepared with some response or information to mitigate the impact of the situation.

Preparation is everything. And it's not just limited to knowing the documents and facts of the case.

Believe it or not, "preparation" also includes the simplest of things, like preparing a list of questions you want to ask a witness and knowing where your questions are written down; having an extra pen or two, a pad of paper, a calculator, and being able to find, in a matter of moments, any exhibits you may wish to use. It even includes the simple act of remembering to turn off your cell phone before you enter the courtroom (more on that later).

2
LEAD DON'T FOLLOW; BE AN ADVOCATE

ANY MATTER IN WHICH YOU BECOME INVOLVED SHOULD BE DRIVEN BY YOU, AND THE PLAN THAT YOU AND YOUR CLIENT LAY OUT TO ACCOMPLISH THEIR GOALS.

You didn't become a lawyer to file lawsuits or draft threatening letters just because your client believes that is what he needs "right now". Nor is it your job to simply answer a letter or lawsuit just because some other lawyer sent a letter or filed an action against your client.

Lawyers are not supposed to simply start lawsuits, do research, and write threatening letters. Half of what an effective attorney does is plan, strategize, and think about how best to accomplish the clients' goals.

Lawyering is about understanding that your clients possess certain strengths and weaknesses, both of which need to be marshaled and made *part of a plan* on the client's behalf. But if you fall into the trap of making knee-jerk reactions to your adversary's every move, you will just end up spending a lot of your time, and your clients' money, *reacting to some other* lawyer's plan.

You do not want to be the attorney who follows someone else's lead; no lawyer should fall into the "my-adversary-did-this-so-I'm-going-to-do-that" trap. To be truly effective, any matter in which you become involved should be driven by you and the plan that you and your client lay out to accomplish their goals. This is what I mean when I say, *"Lead don't follow; be an advocate"*.

If you entered into the practice of law just to make as much money as you can, or to blow your own horn—or if you care more about yourself than becoming a champion of your client—then you will remain a poor advocate. Running your professional life on such a course will rarely provide counsel of any real value to your clients. And if your clients do not perceive that you are taking action that directly benefits them and their causes, your business will ultimately suffer.

Be a leader and advocate for your clients' causes. If you do that, it will be noticed. And that, in turn, will help your business grow. Happy clients refer business.

3
ATTORNEYS OF ALL STRIPES

A PERSON WITH AN INNER MORAL COMPASS, AND A MODICUM OF COMPASSION, WILL BE A BETTER ADVISER AND MORE PASSIONATE ADVOCATE THAN A BRILLIANT STRATEGIST TRYING TO FIGURE OUT ALL THE LEGAL ANGLES AND SHORTCUTS.

There are many kinds of attorneys in this world. By this I'm not referring to various areas of practice, nor do I refer to nationality, race, gender, training or any like matter. Instead, I refer to the way in which attorneys approach their practice, and to their relationship with their clients.

I want to focus here on two different kinds of lawyers:

One of them takes the time, and makes the effort, to listen to, and understand, what his client is telling him. And from the start, he or she is trying to appreciate the situation or problems from the *client's perspective*. This lawyer is already thinking about how he can help the client with the problems he faces.

The other kind of attorney is almost solely focused on his business. He or she is calculating which steps are involved in taking on the case, how successful it may prove to be, and asking themselves, "*Is this worth it to get involved here?*"

If you're beginning your own law practice, the latter mindset is not a good place to start...at least not if that is all you're thinking about. In fact, if the lawyer's own well-being (financial or otherwise) is all he or she is thinking about, it's not going to lead to a good ending either. Of course, the "law business" is a business, and collecting fees is among the most important things one can focus on. Indeed, most of us do have to pay attention to making money because without paying clients, you will be of little use to yourself or your family unless a) you are independently wealthy, or b) you're a salaried employee of the government or some agency, company, firm or organization.

I believe that a person with a good inner moral compass, and a modicum of compassion for the plight of others, will be a better adviser and more passionate advocate for the client than the brilliant strategist simply figuring out all the legal angles and shortcuts. Ben Franklin is supposed to have said, "*If you watch the pennies, the dollars will take care of themselves*". Good advice. I believe that if you take care of the client's needs, your monetary needs will be met. And, in the long run, your business will grow as your reputation as a fine, effective lawyer grows.

4
BEWARE THE LAW OF HOLES

CLIENT EXCUSES FOR NON-PAYMENT WILL VARY FROM THE TRITE TO THE ELABORATE. BUT IF YOU GET INTO A HOLE, STOP DIGGING.

The Law of Holes is used to describe a situation common to attorneys everywhere: The client promises payment but the check never seems to arrive. And every day that passes, you are no doubt putting in more time and effort for the client (digging the hole), so that when your client sends some payment—usually less than all of the sum owed—that money will cover a smaller and smaller percentage of what you are now owed.

What's worse, as you continue digging, you are sure to be told every story in the book. Excuses for non-payment vary from the trite: "*I just now mailed the check*"...to the elaborate: "*The guy who owes me a lot of money is in Europe and comes back on Tuesday*"...or, "*I just finished this small job for a guy and I will get paid next week*". For each lie (for that's what they usually are), it will likely be followed by others that will likely sound something like this: "*The guy only had half of what he owed me, and I had to pay my daughter's tuition, but I will be getting the rest next week*"...or, "*I went to pick up the check and I told him to leave my envelope with his doorman and he forgot, but I will see him next week*".

I have lived through situations like these too many times. And whether you bill by the hour or on a flat-fee, almost every practitioner I know has heard similar tales.

Unless you are very confident that your client is going to prevail in the suit or the claim you are handling, and that any settlement judgment you recover will be collected, I advise you to drop the case, drop the client, and get ready to *not* be paid. Worse, be ready to be accused of all kinds of evil things by this client who has done nothing but praise you up to this point for the great job you are doing and for sticking by him.

Ignore the threats and comments. If there is a case pending in which you are the attorney of record, and the client gets further and further behind, I advise that you make the Motion to get out of the case. Do whatever you have to do to extricate yourself from the situation. It is far better to move on and represent someone you feel good about representing, particularly if with another client you *will* be getting paid.

5
ATTEND COURT CONFERENCES

IF YOU HAVE AN IMPORTANT CASE OR CLIENT, TREAT EVERY INITIAL COURT CONFERENCE (AND ANY OF IMPORTANCE THAT FOLLOW) AS AN IMPORTANT STEP IN THE TRIAL PROCESS.

If you are now, or will become a litigation lawyer, there is no doubt that you will be called upon to attend conferences before the Court.

Conferences are held for many reasons. Most frequently they occur to keep the Court apprised of where your matter stands; or to determine whether there are discovery issues between the parties that need to be resolved; or whether there is a possibility for settlement; and, of course, if there has been no settlement, to schedule a trial. Some judges will also seek conferences with counsel to discuss planned motions, or motions presently pending before them.

Most attorneys hold a very dim view of court conferences because too often little is accomplished, and (also too often) much time is wasted traveling to the courthouse, and then waiting hours for the Court to see the parties' counsel.

But there are occasions when these conferences may provide you with an excellent opportunity to meet the Judge handling your case, and that will provide you a brief opportunity to make a good impression on him or her. Leaving a Judge with the impression that you are a consummate professional, intimately familiar with his case, may have lasting value to you. This is particularly true if your adversary treats conferences as most lawyers do...as a waste of time. These lawyers do not prepare for the conferences, and many, if not most lawyers, don't even bother attending them;

they will send an associate in their stead. In jurisdictions like New York, where courthouses are buried in litigation, this attitude is understandable. It is even more understandable if counsel know in advance that a judge will not even be at the conference; instead, leaving the matter to a staff member such as a clerk or law assistant.

But if you have an important case or client, or you practice in a more intimate jurisdiction, my advice is to treat the initial conference (and any of importance that follow) as an important step in the trial process. If you attend the conference and demonstrate concern and a deep understanding of the matter, it may not be to your immediate benefit, or your client's. But it is my belief that if some positive memory or notation in the file was made, it will in some measure stay with the Court, and, work to your benefit.

But here is a situation you want to absolutely avoid:

Sometimes, Courts will offer attorneys the opportunity to skip attending in person and to take part in the conference by telephone. If the conference is going to address *anything* of importance regarding your case, do not accept that opportunity. Show up. You have no idea how much good can come from actually being there. This is especially true if your adversary is not present before the Judge, but rather, he or she simply called into the conference. You have no idea the amount of non-verbal communication that can occur between the Judge and the party(ies) who are present when other counsel is only "present" on the phone. So, your lack of presence might give your adversary a huge advantage. Because if you are the person merely "calling in", you will never know what non-verbal communication has passed between the Court and your adversary.

Do not be the person who takes the easy way out. Yes, it will cost you more time, and your client more money to "be there".

But at the end of the conference, it will be you, and maybe you alone, who will be able to smile and shake the Judge's hand. You will be recalled as the person who came to the Judge because it was a matter of importance to you and to your client.

6

A TIME TO FIGHT AND A TIME TO DEAL

IF YOUR CLIENT IS ON THE RIGHT SIDE OF THE ARGUMENT, IT WILL BE HARD TO EXPLAIN WHY SETTLING MAY STILL BE THE BEST COURSE OF ACTION.

Litigation is nearly always time-consuming and expensive, and it compels lawyers and clients to constantly have discussions about whether the fight is worth it in time and money. In fact, I've had many clients who were patently not in the wrong but who decided to settle (pay off) a claim rather than fight it simply because the cost of defending litigation made defending, *and even winning*, a losing proposition from a financial perspective.

It happens every day in New York, and I'm sure it occurs just as frequently in many other jurisdictions.

The problem is best described this way:

Your client gets sued for, say, $28,000. Your client says something like, "*This is absurd, I don't owe him anything*". But you know that just to defend the claim will take many hours, and, if the case is not resolved relatively quickly, the costs of defending the suit (without any hope that your defense costs will be reimbursed) will equal or even far exceed the sum the matter could be settled for.

Of course, in our adversary system it takes both side's lawyers to recognize the issue, and to desire to try to solve the dispute or problem early and inexpensively. To even start down this road requires that you have a hard conversation with the client at the outset. If your client is on the right side of the argument but is still being sued for a small sum, it will be hard to explain why settling may be his best course of action. But the problem presented here is not just one for the client. It is a problem for you, too.

Because no one, and I mean no one, wins in these circumstances. If the client settles a case by paying money that he felt should never be paid, that client may—consciously or not—hold you responsible for "thinking (or talking) him into it". And, if the matter is not resolved quickly, your client will one day ask you, "*How did my bill for this get to be $25,000?*" What can lead to an even worse situation is when the client insists that he would "rather pay you than give the plaintiff a dime." (*See Section III*).

7
A CAUTION ON TAPING CALLS AND CONVERSATIONS

BECAUSE TAPING CONVERSATIONS RUNS THE RISK OF A POTENTIAL CRIMINAL PROSECUTION, OR POSSIBLE SUSPENSION OR DISBARMENT, GIVE CAREFUL THOUGHT ABOUT UNDERTAKING THAT CONDUCT.

Every state has its own rules regarding when, and whether, surreptitiously taping phone calls or in-person conversations is legal. These rules may also differ in criminal and civil matters, and no lawyer should recommend to any client, or other person working for the lawyer, that conversations be taped in secret without first carefully reading the statutes, regulations, and cases that govern the issue in the applicable jurisdiction.

Lawyers also have to be mindful of the fact that *even if* your particular state allows one party to tape another without that person being aware of it, *the rules governing lawyers' conduct* may differ dramatically. In fact, they may specifically bar the practice by an attorney. In New York, for example, a conversation may be legally recorded if one party to the conversation consents to the taping. But ethical considerations and the disciplinary rules do not allow a lawyer, or anyone acting at the lawyer's direction, to tape another party without that party's knowledge.

Before you espouse advice about what your jurisdiction allows or does not allow, do the necessary research about the laws in your jurisdiction... and double-check the rules that govern the conduct of lawyers specifically. It may even be prohibited for a lawyer to coach a client to tape another without their knowledge—even if the conduct itself would otherwise be legal.

The point is that taped conversations—particularly where one is speaking freely among persons he or she trusts—can provide powerful evidence on the subject of such critical matters as intent, motive, and admissions. But if the price of such evidence is a potential criminal prosecution, or possible suspension or disbarment, one should think long and hard about undertaking that conduct.

Section VII
PREPARING FOR TESTIMONY AND MATTERS OF PRESENTATION

1
OUR ADVERSARY SYSTEM

ONLY BY KNOWING THE OTHER SIDE'S CASE AS WELL OR BETTER THAN YOUR ADVERSARY, CAN YOU GUARD AGAINST BEING TAKEN BY SURPRISE AT THE BARGAINING TABLE, AT A DEPOSITION, OR WORSE, AT TRIAL.

Because we have an "adversary system", it is a trial lawyer's job to not only present their case as best he or she can, but to destroy the other side's case. As our United States Supreme Court said in one opinion, "*...partisan advocacy on both sides of a case will best promote the ultimate objective*" of obtaining justice and equity.

I am aware of a contrary school of thought that holds that the adversary system is actually harmful to the search for truth, and that it distorts facts, tends to keep certain relevant evidence from seeing the light of day, and causes extensive delays in the judicial process.

Like it or not, though, this is the system we have.

If you are involved in a negotiation of a contract dispute, you are doing your job right if you have not only thought out your case for your client, but have also figured out your adversary's best case or best argument. Only by knowing the other side's case as well or better than your adversary, can you best take advantage of their case's weak points and guard against being taken by surprise at the bargaining table, at a deposition, or worse, during a trial. I was always taught to prepare your case as though your adversary is the "best in the business". And, if the day comes when your adversary does raise a major defense, or produces that killer witness you feared he would discover, you will be as prepared as you can be to meet the other side's best arguments because you have thought about them for months. Of course, if your adversary falls short of the mark, you will look that much better.

You may have heard it said before: In the business of lawyering, *preparation is everything.*

It's more true than you know.

The very last thing a good lawyer can afford is to appear to a client, or to a judge, that you seem unprepared, caught off guard, or look baffled or foolish. That one fear is what drives me to do the very best I can. It's not the money—although clearly that's important, too (after all, my law practice is my business not my hobby). But just the thought of me, or my firm, being embarrassed in court by a judge or adversary, or in any meeting, scares the heck out of me. And it should scare you, too.

2

TRIAL SKILLS AND THE VALUE OF SETTLEMENTS

BEING "TRIAL SHY", OR HAVING A REPUTATION FOR NOT PREPARING A SOLID CASE, WILL ONLY GET YOU "LOW BALL" SETTLEMENT OFFERS... WHICH WILL GET EVEN LOWER OVER TIME.

If you are known as a thorough opponent, if you are someone not afraid to take on causes and argue for your side (and/or try cases), your ability to settle any matter on favorable terms *increases*. Your opponents will know that you're not bluffing when you call to try to resolve a matter early in the game *"before it gets expensive"* (meaning it will cost both sides a lot of money to litigate).

But if you are "trial shy", or you get a reputation for not being willing to put in the time to prepare a solid argument or case, your settlement discussions will, at best, lead to "low ball" offers (which will get even lower over time). Why? Because your adversaries will learn that if they push the case hard and long enough, the more likely it is that you will settle as you get closer to having to try the case. So, I strongly suggest that you develop the skills and the confidence to speak up, and speak out, for yourself and your client.

Don't worry if you have qualms about speaking in a courtroom, or generally speaking in public. You can become comfortable in that role over time.

Here's my suggestion:

Whenever you are not absolutely swamped with work, get to the nearest courthouse and watch any trial for a while. In fact, watch several. You don't have to spend all day. But over time, do attend parts of several trials, and spend your time watching other lawyers. What you will learn is that the quality of lawyering in most cases will lead you to this conclusion: "*I can do that! I can even do better than that.*" Moreover, with every argument you make in court, with each jury you select, with every opening statement *you* make, and with every appeal you argue, your speaking and trial skills will improve...often dramatically, because you will have become more at ease. There is never a downside to speaking out for yourself and your client. You just have to believe in what you are saying (or at least act like you believe it). Oh, and know the rules of evidence.

3
LOOSE LIPS SINK SHIPS

DO NOT DISCUSS ANY ASPECT OF YOUR CASE, OR ONGOING PROCEEDINGS, WITH ANYONE WHEN OTHERS ARE PRESENT AND MIGHT POSSIBLY HEAR YOU.

Just as with deposition testimony, sometimes there are rules in some jurisdictions that prohibit or limit discussion in the courthouse between lawyers and witnesses during trials. In addition, some judges have their own rules on this topic.

Whether such rules exist or not in your jurisdiction, do not—repeat, *do not*—discuss any aspect of your case or the ongoing proceedings with your witness, or anyone else for that matter, when other people are present and might possibly hear you...even if there seems almost no chance that someone connected to the case might overhear the conversation.

I have heard horror stories about how very significant cases were compromised by lawyers having what one assumed was a confidential communication overheard by a judge's law clerk, a juror, or an adverse party. In fact, in a courthouse elevator, I once overheard a near-whispered conversation between a lawyer and client about some perceived difficulties they were having with the jury. The elevator was very crowded that day, and when it emptied on the ground floor, the lawyer turned pale because he recognized that one of his own jurors had been standing at the rear of the car. Whatever the lawyer said to his client that day, he certainly did not want any juror to hear it! I can't say what damage was done by that one overheard conversation, but I do know the lawyer did not prevail in the case.

It is also true that in jurisdictions where proceedings are audio and/or videotaped you should assume that the machine is recording at all times. So, do not speak about your case in what may look like an empty courtroom either. Why take chances? Follow this simple rule: No talking in elevators, bathrooms or hallways. No talking unless you are absolutely sure the conversation is completely private.

4
YOUR CLIENT AS A WITNESS

EVERY CLIENT NEEDS TO HAVE AT LEAST ONE LONG CONVERSATION WITH HIS OR HER LAWYER ABOUT EVERYTHING THAT COMES INTO PLAY WHEN "TELLING HIS STORY".

How can one become a credible witness for his own cause? Well, it matters greatly whether your client is going to be a witness in a courtroom proceeding (at a hearing or a trial); a witness in a less formal administrative hearing, arbitration or mediation proceeding; or, perhaps, in a deposition. Every client, unless they are extremely litigious, or are used to speaking in front of rooms full of people, needs to have at least one long conversation with his or her lawyer about everything that comes into play when "telling his story" in a legal manner. This discussion should include everything from "atmospherics" to proper "demeanor", and will have to address your client's questions and to allay any fears he may have about testifying. In short, you need to bring your client to a level of fluency with the facts of his matter, and a level of comfort with the situation, so as to best achieve his story being believed. Different approaches work for different circumstances, and I try to break them down in the sections that follow.

5
JUDGES ARE JUST PEOPLE, TOO

IT CAN'T HURT TO TAKE ADVANTAGE OF THE CHANCE TO SPEAK TO JUDGES IN SOCIAL SETTINGS. IT'S A GOOD FEELING IF YOU CAN WALK INTO A COURTROOM AND BE KNOWN TO THE JUDGE BY YOUR FIRST NAME.

A young lawyer I know reminded me that newer associates in some firms are sometimes given the opportunity to attend, at the firm's expense, bar association or law group functions (luncheons, dinner meetings, etc.) where judges are known to attend. But whether or not the firm is footing the bill, it cannot hurt to take advantage of the chance to speak to judges in social settings. You never know what you might find in common to discuss, and where such meetings might lead. It is always a good feeling if you can walk into a courtroom and be known to the Judge by your first name. Understanding that judges are just people, too, is important if you are going to appear in court as part of your career.

One of the best trial lawyers I ever knew once told me, "*Never fear the man or woman wearing the black robe. They eat, drink, go home at night, and have family problems just like us ... because they are us. The worst they can do to you is to hold you in contempt, and if they do, someone will come and get you out*".

I always try to be respectful to any Court I appear before, but sometimes when arguments get heated, emotions sometimes run high, and I admit to having been threatened with contempt. It's not so bad. In fact, among some lawyers, it's a sort of badge of honor because it shows you are pressing your client's case to the limit. Remember, though: Never be intentionally disrespectful to any Judge in his or her courtroom. It's rarely worth it.

6
PREPARING THE CLIENT FOR DEPOSITION TESTIMONY

TELL THE CLIENT TO ANSWER ONLY THE QUESTION ASKED. EVEN IF THEY'RE ASKED IF THEY'RE WEARING A WATCH, THEY SHOULD NOT LOOK AT IT AND TELL THE LAWYER THE TIME... BECAUSE THAT WAS NOT THE QUESTION.

If your client is being deposed in his own case, and has never been deposed before, it is very important to put them at ease about the testimony he is about to give. Even if your client is a deposition "pro" (like someone in a large company who has testified in many matters), prepare your client anyway, as every lawyer has his own view on how depositions should be handled.

For many matters, the deposition is the first time your client will meet your adversary. And impressions made at that first meeting could prove vastly important to the rest of your case.

There is little doubt that the adversary will have been told what a bad guy your client is, what a liar he is, and that he is not to be trusted. Your adversary will likely have been told all kind of bad things about your client and why he was sued; or why your client commenced a meritless suit against your adversary's client. Your goal, in any deposition, is to destroy that impression and make your witness appear truthful, professional, well-mannered, in command of the facts of his case, and in your theory of the case (meaning, the plan you have crafted to make your case in court).

The two most important things about a deposition is (a) to leave your adversary with the impression that your client will be believed by the Judge, jury, arbitrators, or whomever is deciding the case; and (b) to ensure that all the elements of your cause of action are laid bare (or at least so much of them that are asked about by the attorney). This will best be achieved by making your client as comfortable as possible with the process and the manner in which it will take place. For that reason, you should always give your client a preview of what to expect in a deposition generally, and in your case specifically. The former part can be shortened substantially if the client has been deposed before. But both topics are important, however, particularly if your client is new to litigation. Having a thorough but friendly conversation about what will occur is a good way to "take the edge off" of a client nervous about testifying.

If the deposition will take place in your office, prepare your client in the room where the deposition will actually be held.

If the deposition is to take place at the courthouse, or in another lawyer's office, take the time to explain the way the room is laid out. Make sure your client understands that even if the deposition is taken at the courthouse, that no Judge and no jury will be present; that parties will be sitting informally around a table, and that someone will be taking down *everything* they say. Or that the proceedings will be audio or videotaped. The point is to make sure your client understands that everything said will be recorded...and will be under oath.

Because there will be a transcript, the client must be told that his words will appear on paper, in cold black-and-white, and any inflection in their voice will be lost. Sarcasm, jokes and light banter, always read very differently than what was heard when the words were spoken, so it should be totally avoided.

Let's go over your client's conduct at the deposition:

I tell clients that a deposition—at least in State courts—can be a very long, drawn-out (even a multi-day) experience, or it can be very short. I follow this up by saying that our goal is to "control" the deposition, and to try to limit the deposition's length and scope. The rules of the game, as I explain them, is to show the questioner total respect, as he or she is just another working man (or woman) doing their job.

Even aggressive lawyers, abusive questioners, and those who act incredulous at every answer uttered, can be "controlled" if your client follows rules you clearly lay out for testifying at a deposition. The same tactics can work well at trial during cross-examination, but more on that later.

People in a heightened emotional state tend to blurt out answers rather than think out answers before speaking. So, one key to controlling a client's deposition is to tell your client that—*no matter what!*—to keep their temper and emotions in check. If an attorney gets a rise out of the witness, he will relentlessly pursue the tone or topic that triggered the emotional response.

A second tried-and-true method for controlling the pace of a deposition is to make the client promise you that he will listen to the *entire* question before responding. And that every single response should be guided by the principle that a witness should always use the shortest number of words possible to fully and directly answer the question asked... *and only the question asked.*

Why? Two reasons:

First, the more your client talks, the more things he is likely to say that will lead to even more questions by the adversary. If you explain this to the client, he will likely want to keep his answers clipped. The other reason is that the only purpose for a deposition is to enable your adversary to use it—or portions of it—at a later motion or at trial. Long answers, or flowing conversation, are to be avoided as both tend to be more descriptive and more detailed. If your adversary is reading that transcript at trial, or playing the tape, he is doing it because words used by your client do not help your client's case. Keep it short. It makes the adversary's job much harder to find descriptive explanations to use against your client.

I repeat: tell the client to answer *only* the question asked. Even if they're asked, "*Are you wearing a watch?*, they should not look at their watch and tell the lawyer the time because that was *not* the question. Also, your client must be admonished to never, ever guess at an answer. A guess helps no one. If your client doesn't know the answer because they were not in a position to know, saying they do not know is a perfectly fine response.

Another hint for controlling the tempo and tenor of your client's deposition:

Make your client promise to silently count off at least two full seconds *after* the full question is asked and understood before responding. This is intended to make the client think of the question asked, and to answer *only* that question (with as few words as possible). But it has a second, more profound effect when actually followed. If your client promises to do this—and *does* do it—no matter how angry or loud or quickly the lawyer poses questions, your client is controlling the tempo of the questioning and the answers, and is slowing the conversation down. By the way, if the deposition is being recorded by a stenographer or reporter, the pauses will not even appear in the transcript. And if there is an audio or videotape your client will appear thoughtful not obstructive; a fact that cannot hurt you. I have seen some very frustrated attorneys look foolish in videos when they try to jar a client but fail to do so.

Many attorneys also tell their clients that the answer "*I don't remember*" is also a perfectly acceptable. I disagree with this position if the topic is critical to your case.

An "I-don't-remember" answer will allow an attorney questioning your client later at a trial, or at a hearing, to say something like, "*Mr. Jones, you just testified that when the truck stopped in front of you, it stopped short and there were no brake lights on. But when I asked you the same question 15 months ago during a deposition, you said you could not recall if there were brake lights on*". This will no doubt be followed by all manner of incredulous mannerisms and questions about your client's amazing ability to better recall facts further in time from the events than he could at an earlier time. "*You mean your memory is actually better today than it was 15 months ago, a time much closer to the event?*" The implication is that your client is embellishing, and no matter how much the client says, "*Now, I remember…*", the Judge or jury will also question your witness' credibility. Because as every lawyer will remind the Judge and/or jury, everyone knows that memories fade over time.

A better way to handle that situation at the deposition is to refer to something that might help your client recall. He or she might say something like, "*I know I told the police officer what I saw, and he wrote down what I said that day. If I could see his report, I could better recall*". Or your client might say, "*I texted my brother after the accident as I was going to be late to a meeting with him. I believe that if I could see that message I might recall*". In this way, you have done two things, both good, for your case. First, you have opened the door for your client to say, "*I remember because I reviewed the document before testifying.*" Or, even if he still does not remember, you may well get the statement in through the evidence rule governing past recollection recorded; a rule of evidence used in virtually every jurisdiction. (You just have to look up what foundation questions you have to ask your witness to get a document and testimony admitted this way).

A few thoughts about your client's appearance at the deposition:

Many clients will ask you what they should wear. Your client should be dressed "business-appropriate", and he or she should be comfortable. If your client does not ask you the question, you should remind your client what you expect him or her to wear. What to actually wear depends on many factors, the most important of which are: Is the deposition going to be videotaped; and what is your client's line of work. Whether your client is a professional, a shoe salesman, a mechanic, or anything in-between, I believe he or she should not treat the deposition as a "day off", and that he or she should dress as they would for any business meeting. If the deposition is going to be videotaped, however, you want your client to appear as he or she would at trial before a Judge and jury.

7
DEPOSITIONS: SOME TRICKS OF THE TRADE

WHETHER IT'S A DEPOSITION, SETTLEMENT CONFERENCE, ARBITRATION, MEDIATION OR TRIAL, YOUR CLIENT SHOULD NEVER "FILL IN THE SILENCE".

Any time two people converse, or when a client testifies, there is an urge to fill any periods of silence. Make sure your client does not feel so compelled. When words fill silences—which are often *intentionally created by lawyers* to see what the witness will say—your client's extra words will only serve to form the basis for more questions.

As I have said in the previous essay, your client should wait for every question to be asked in full, to pause and *then* answer the question asked, or, if need be, to ask that it be clarified. Once the client has answered, to make sure he or she understands that their job is to say nothing and simply wait, no matter how long it takes to hear the next full question. Whether during a deposition, or taking part in a settlement conference, arbitration, mediation or trial, filling in silences never helps the story. On the other hand, when juries or Judges are present, long pauses between questions will always be interpreted as a sign that the questioner is not prepared to follow up, and that is a good thing for you.

Experienced adversaries don't always ask, *"Did you meet with your lawyer before you testified?"* This is particularly true if they know you are the sort of lawyer who prepares his clients well. However, the question is asked often enough to warrant a brief mention here.

If your client is asked, in any form, *"Did you meet with your lawyer before you testified?"* or, *"Did you review what would be said here today with your attorney?"* your client should answer honestly. And the answer should sound something like this: *"Of course I met with my lawyer. I had to go over everything with him because he did not live this case as I did. I had to tell him all about the matter"*. And if pressed, their answer should sound something like this, *"Well, my lawyer did say to be brief and be honest. He said (name of state) jurors are typically really smart people, and that they will know the truth when they hear it."* A response of this sort tends to resonate because it elevates the client and the lawyer, and signals to an adversary that the witness has been well-prepared, and that he had better ask the rest of his questions carefully. At trial, the responses I'm suggesting have even more value. Because even if the Judge rolls his or her eyes, a response along these lines tells the jury that you and your client are confident in your case, and you respect them to reach a good verdict in this case.

Can you discuss the case with your client during the deposition?

When you are attending an important deposition, or you are actually on trial for your client's cause, your client will want to discuss everything that happens in the proceedings with you. In the case of depositions, you need to check the local ethical and court rules governing the jurisdiction you are in. Some rules (or Judges) prohibit all conversation between the client and his counsel while the deposition is ongoing; others limit it in some significant ways. Know the rules. Losing a case, or having important testimony stricken because you did not prepare the client, or because you breached some rule governing attorney-client conversation, can be very costly and is avoidable if you know the rules in advance.

8
GETTING READY FOR A TRIAL, ARBITRATION, OR HEARING

YOUR WITNESS MUST EXHIBIT COMFORT, ASSURANCE, AND KNOWLEDGE OF THE FACTS; IF THEY'RE AFRAID TO MEET THE EYES OF THE JUDGE OR JURY, ALL THE BEST-REHEARSED TESTIMONY IN THE WORLD WILL BE FOR NOTHING.

A trial or hearing is the "big show". It's *the* event that you and the client have prepared for, and it is likely the sole opportunity to convince the trier of fact that your client should be believed and should win.

Because your client is likely to be a complete stranger to the Judge and/or jury, it's your job to make sure they come to know, to like, and to believe your client in what little time he or she has to make a good impression. For this reason, I always tell my witnesses that I want them to relax in the courtroom, and to relate their story as if telling it to me in my office, or to their friends in their own living room. Sometimes I will take them to a courtroom before the trial, and let them watch a witness take the stand in another case. And, if I can find an empty and open courtroom, I will encourage the client to actually sit in the witness chair and get a feel for it. I also point out that whether the chair is not fixed to the floor, or whether it swivels, that the witness should face the person to whom they are telling their story, and to meet their eyes, as best he can.

This little preparation has a side benefit: it will help make *you, too,* comfortable in the courtroom.

When the day comes for the actual trial, it will feel familiar for both you and the client to be facing each other in that same setting.

Truth is conveyed not by words alone, but also by demeanor and mannerisms. If a witness is afraid to meet the eyes of the Judge or jury, all the best-rehearsed testimony in the world will be for nothing. Your witness must exhibit comfort, assurance, and knowledge of the facts. He or she should exude confidence but never arrogance. If they mumble, or speak with downcast eyes, he or she will be perceived as being deceptive or lacking in confidence, and hence, lacking in credibility.

Court dress code:

Don't try to "dress down" a multi-millionaire client, or have someone like a high-powered hedge fund manager wear ripped jeans and work boots to appear like a "regular guy". It will not appear authentic to any Judge or jury, and the one thing you want your client to exude from every pore is...honesty.

Demeanor in the courtroom:

I have been in dozens of courtrooms in New York and New Jersey, and virtually every one of them has a sign outside the courtroom doors that says something like, *"Please, before you enter the courtroom, turn off your cell phone."* About two years ago, I tried a case in New Jersey before a Judge who was known for his no-nonsense approach to trials. Just as the Court was calling the case to begin, my adversary's cell phone rang. We were in small courtroom, so the jarring brrrrrrriiinngging seemed even louder, and no one... certainly not the Judge...could miss where it was coming from. My worthy adversary scrambled to find and silence his phone, and the few minutes or so it took him to do it seemed to go on much longer than it actually did. You could tell that the Judge was really pissed (this is not a legal term, but you get the idea). But that wasn't the end of it. Later, after a long morning session, when we returned from lunch, the Judge said to my opponent, "*Mr. ____, I trust you are ready to continue with your cross-examination?*" And, you guessed it, even before the lawyer could say, "*Yes, Judge, I am*", his cell phone erupted again! This time the Judge was near apoplectic. Let me tell you, it's a great position to be in when your adversary is so sloppy—even on the small things—that he makes you look great by default.

When you stand before a Judge in his or her courtroom, they expect your full attention, and they expect you to be professional in all respects...and, yes, they expect that you will be prepared. My adversary eventually learned to shut off his phone before coming into the courtroom. But you can benefit from this story. Don't you be the lawyer who draws the ire of the Court for the things that are easily avoidable. Trying cases, particularly against well-prepared adversaries is hard enough. Be prepared, be professional...and turn off your cell phone.

9
ON DIRECT EXAMINATION

WHEN I PREPARE A WITNESS FOR THE STORY THEY'RE GOING TO TELL, I WANT THEM TO TELL IT SLOWLY, AS THOUGH IT WAS ON A MOVIE FILM STRIP...FRAME-BY-FRAME, IMAGE BY IMAGE.

Some helpful points on telling your client's story:

A lawyer may not lead his own witness (at least not for long, if one does try to get away with it). You, as the lawyer, just cannot tell the story and have your client say something like, *"Yes, that's right"* or, *"Yes, that's the way it happened"*.

So how do you introduce your client, and his or her story, to the jury or Judge? In a word: slowly.

When I prepare the witness for the story they are going to tell, I tell my client that I want their story to come out slowly and in detail. To do this, I use the analogy of a movie film strip. A film strip, I explain, contains a series of many hundreds of still pictures that, when taken together, show a moving image. I want my client to tell their story frame-by-frame, image by image. I want the jury to hear the story as though they were watching a compelling movie. And I want the first four or five minutes of that "movie" to be about nothing except who the client is, what their family is like, where they live, what their educational background is, and what their work experience has been.

Now, with the film strip concept firmly implanted—and with the trier of the facts knowing something about the witness—I take the client through the story frame by frame. We describe the events that led him or her to this very day in this very courtroom before this Judge or jury.

The witness already knows which exhibits and evidence I

am going to use because we have practiced this testimony more than once in my office. He already knows what he has to say to get exhibits into evidence (to properly lay the foundation for evidence), because I have explained the rules for getting exhibits into evidence, or what are the proper "foundation questions".

And, with each piece of important evidence, we linger over the details, and I give the witness a chance to expound on his or her story while they *talk to the jury*. If your witness gets too far ahead of themselves, as witnesses often will, I will take the witness back over things that should be described more slowly or in greater detail. You want the jury to live the events as your client *relives* the events. And we continue in this fashion until the entire film strip (or as much of it as this witness has to say) has been unspooled.

The point of this is to give the jury a complete, well-rounded picture of who it is sitting before them (and I usually remind the jury at the end of the case that, in weighing a case, it's not just the story that is important, but, equally important—perhaps more important—*who* is telling the story). So when the Judge instructs the jury on weighing a witness's credibility, your words should play into this instruction, bolstering their trust in you, and hopefully, by extension, in your client.

10
SOME CAUTIONS ABOUT DIRECT TESTIMONY

AN OBJECTION MEANS A CLIENT SHOULD IMMEDIATELY STOP TALKING; THAT IS, TO NOT ANSWER, TO NOT ARGUE, AND TO AWAIT THE JUDGE'S RULING AND INSTRUCTION ON WHETHER OR NOT TO ANSWER.

Judges have the right and the power to ask questions of your witness at any time…and for any reason. Some questions may be objectionable, but that's another issue, and—at a sidebar—you will want to protect your trial record, and object to the Court's questioning if necessary. Make sure your witness prepares for the possibility that questions may be asked of him from the bench, otherwise it might throw them off-balance.

Instruct your witness that if the Judge does ask questions, they should turn and face the Judge and refer to him or her as *"Your Honor"* or *"Judge"*. Furthermore, your witness should listen to the entire question without interruption, and to make sure they understand before responding. Tell them that if they do not understand the question, they should say so. But above all, your witness must remain courteous and confident with the Judge.

Other than loud objections, the other possible surprises for which many attorneys fail to prepare clients is an adversary's request for a *voir dire* (a term meaning "speak the truth") right in the middle of direct testimony. If a Court allows a *voir dire* of the witness, the Judge is giving your adversary the opportunity to ask your client direct questions in the middle of your practiced examination. These questions are allowed for the purpose of testing the admissibility of evidence (usually documentary evidence, but it could be demonstrative evidence or other kinds), and, if it occurs, your client should be prepared to address the issues. Otherwise, the interruption of the flow of the dance—or act—you have created can really break the timing and tempo you practiced, and it will rattle your client.

Dealing with objections:

All the client needs to know is that if there is an objection (whether by your adversary on direct examination, or by you on cross), the witness should immediately stop talking, to not answer or argue, and to wait for the Judge's ruling and instruction on whether to answer or not. You can tell the client that asking to have the question re-read is okay, as the interruption may have caused him or her to forget the question asked, and you always only want an answer to the question actually asked.

A further word of caution with regard to the conduct of Judges:

A Judge can help or hurt your case, not only by what he or she says, but also by non-verbal communications that can easily signal to a jury what the Judge is thinking about your case or witness. For example, the Judge's rolling of his eyes during a witness' answer, or his incredulous, *can-you-believe-this* look on his face could be read by the jury as commentary on the veracity of the witness. Conceivably, these or other reactions from the Judge could kill everything you have worked for.

If something like this does occur, you must ask for a sidebar and make a record of your objection to it. If you are denied the sidebar, make the record at the first chance you get, stating why you asked for the sidebar when your witness was on the stand. Trust me when I say that your adversary will not help you with this. Even if your adversary is a "friend", he or she will deny that he saw anything improper. Nevertheless, you have to tell the Judge (out of the hearing of the jury) that while you are absolutely sure that he intended no such thing, his actions strongly conveyed his disbelief and or dislike of your client. You should further ask the Judge upon the jury's return to instruct the jurors that, if he made any gesture that may have conveyed any impression that he felt one way or another about the testimony of any witness, that the jurors should ignore it. A good Judge will add, if you ask, that he meant no such thing. However, most Judges will simply deny that anything occurred, and even deny the mid-trial instruction, saying that the general jury charges at the end of the case will cover the Judge's rulings and actions.

So, while you might not get the instruction you seek, at least you put an objection in the record. If you truly believe that the Judge has hurt you, you might wish to weigh saying something on the issue directly to the jurors in summation. It's about all you can do. It is completely proper in a summation to remind the jury that they, not you, not your adversary, and not the Judge, are the sole determiners of both credibility and the facts.

One more note: If the Judge should appear to signal that he disbelieves your adversary's client, the roles of the attorneys I just outlined will be completely reversed, and you will have the opportunity to deny that you saw anything improper in the Judge's conduct when your adversary later objects to it.

11
PREPARING THE CLIENT FOR CROSS-EXAMINATION

YOUR WITNESS'S DEMEANOR AND TESTIMONY SHOULD DIFFER SIGNIFICANTLY FOR CROSS-EXAMINATION THAN FOR DIRECT.

When preparing a witness for his testimony, you have to prepare him for the questions that you expect your adversary to ask. Your client should be instructed that you will have a right to object...and may do so at any time. And if they hear an objection from you, they should not answer the question, and should await further instruction from either the Court or from you.

In court, your witness' demeanor and testimony should be very different for cross-examination than it is for direct. No longer should the witness be "conversational" or expansive in his answers as he was in response to your questioning.

In general, inform your client that on cross-examination that clear, short answers are better than long; that no matter what, they should try to maintain their composure and to remain courteous at all times. Boiled down to its basics, the rule of the day should be, "*Yes, sir*" and "*No, sir*". And the second rule is that a credible witness does not argue with the lawyer for the other side; he should meet his or her eyes when answering.

Also, remind your client to look over at the jury from time to time, just as your client would if they would if they were sitting on the client's living room sofa. It is OK to tell your client that if, during cross-examination your adversary shouts, argues or yells, your witness can softly and simply ask, "*Why are you shouting?*" The jury might even laugh themselves, forcing the lawyer to lower his voice or he might even continue with a tirade and will make a fool of himself if the witness remains calm. The witness should also be told that laughing is fine if something is funny. A jury that laughs along with, *and not at*, your client is a good sign. It reveals that the jury is listening and feels a certain affinity with him.

Finally, a jury awards no points to an argumentative or smart-aleck witness. No one likes an arrogant witness, or a know-it-all.

Your client needs to know that the jury is *always* watching him and he must act always—not just on the witness stand—as though the trial is the most important thing in his life while he is in the courtroom. As I've said before, courtroom demeanor is important. *Very* important.

Section VIII
COMMENTS ON DRAFTSMANSHIP

1
WRITE SIMPLY AND CLEARLY

THERE IS NO REASON TO USE A $10 WORD WHEN A $5 WORD WILL DO; SOMETHING IS WRONG IF YOUR CLIENT CANNOT READ HIS OWN AGREEMENT AND KNOW EXACTLY WHAT IT SAYS.

If you are retained to assist with making a deal of some kind, but also to "document it", your job is to make damn sure that the papers your client signs *clearly* state what your client's agreement is. Too many lawyers try to impress clients, Judges, and their adversaries (and maybe themselves, too), by drafting huge agreements, using large words, erudite language, and attaching all sorts of schedules and exhibits.

I admit, some deals cry out for this kind of draftsmanship, at least when it comes to schedules and attachments. Complex real estate deals and business mergers, and asset sales, all have to be fully fleshed out, or a third party who is reading the deal terms may never know what was meant to be included or excluded, and/or exactly what was agreed to. But most everyday business agreements that small law firms, or sole practitioners will be asked to draft, do not require this kind of excessive treatment, and the general rule in my firm is "simplicity whenever possible".

As I mentioned earlier in this book, many years ago, I represented a midsized North Jersey bank. It loaned tens of millions of dollars a year to real estate developers and businessmen of all kinds. This bank hired some of the largest, most respected law firms in the region to negotiate and document these mega-development deals, and they paid their transactional lawyers handsomely in the process. And the agreements were impressive to behold; cross-indexed, leather-bound volumes with tables of contents and voluminous exhibits. All lined up on the bank's general counsel's office bookshelf, some of these contracts looked like *"The Complete Works of Chaucer"*. I'm not kidding. In fact, one contract alone, documenting a complex real estate development transaction, might have taken up two shelves in one of the bank's conference rooms.

One day, one the bank's best, most well-heeled clients defaulted under the terms of one of these mega-deals and litigation ensued. The case, not handled by my firm, carried on for years at great expense to both sides. As the bank's attorneys had made matters so complex in their effort to cover every conceivable issue, no Judge could (or would) read the beautiful, leather-bound agreement to determine who was right on the particular matter complained of! Experts were called in, a trial was held, and appeals were taken. So much time and money was spent in this endeavor that everyone but the trial lawyers ended up being "losers".

When at all possible, I urge my associates and legal assistants to write short, clear, practical documents.

If, barring some learning disability, the client cannot read his own agreement and know exactly what it says, something is wrong. And if a Judge cannot read that same agreement and decide who was supposed to do what, the lawyers have somehow failed. Simply put, there is no reason to use a $10 word or phrase when a $5 word will do.

I have witnessed some very talented attorneys arguing over the meaning of a contract term before a Judge on behalf of their clients. These lawyers are great orators, and can be very persuasive. Still, in such a situation, it is not the lawyer's skills that will persuade a Judge charged with enforcing a contract, it is the Judge's understanding (or perhaps the lack of it) that will govern how the

Court rules. No amount of fine argument skills can confuse the Judge, if he is reviewing a crystal-clear contract clause. And when your adversary is claiming an agreement that you drafted says one thing and the Judge looks down from his bench at your adversary and says, "*Counselor, it says right here in black and white that . . .*" Validation from the Court of something that you drafted simply and clearly is a thing of beauty to behold. Let other lawyers try to dazzle and impress with their "legalese". Courts love reading documents; they love it even more when the language is simple, direct and clear. It makes their job so much easier. If you know any Judges, ask them what they prefer.

2
MISTAKES: THEY HAPPEN, SO LEARN FROM THEM

IF YOU TRY TO ACCOMPLISH MULTIPLE TASKS SIMULTANEOUSLY, SOMETHING IS LIKELY TO SUFFER...WITH EMBARRASSING CONSEQUENCES

We learn from our mistakes. After more than 30 years in legal practice, I still make my share of them. And so does every lawyer I know (which is one reason why they call law a "practice"). Still, if given the choice, I would rather learn from someone else's mistakes. It's a lot less painful and time-consuming, which, as I have stated earlier, is the main purpose of this book.

Do yourself a huge favor: Spend the time to get it right the first time, whatever "it" is. To have to do something over—to have to correct your mistake—takes *way more* time and effort than doing something right the first time. For example, if you have two phones ringing at the same time, and there is someone sitting across from you, and another person appears at your office door trying to get your attention, it is easy to mess up something even as simple as an email you're in the middle of drafting. It's also easy to sign letters that have the wrong address or that contain silly, sometimes embarrassing mistakes.

A personal example:

One day, our office had to mail out some 20 letters to various counsel, parties, and the Court. I had written the letters, and had given the job of making sure the right letters and enclosures were in the correct envelopes to a trusted long-time assistant. But I was in the middle of a scene not unlike the one described in the paragraph above. Too much was going on. And when the letters were brought for my signature, I hastily signed them and told her to please "get them out". Sadly, I did not take the extra five or ten minutes to check that the names that appeared after "*Dear* ___" matched the addressee. Nor did I double-check that all the parties' names and addresses were correct, or that all of the letters that needed to be in that stack of letters were in fact there.

The result? Not good.

It looks totally unprofessional when a letter addressed to "*Dave Smith*" reads "*Dear Steve*". Worse yet, several of the envelopes were sent back as "undeliverable" because they didn't have the right address.

This, frankly, is inexcusable.

I had to go back and duplicate the work, and spend even more time making the appropriate apologies. As things go, this example was for a small, minor matter. But large mistakes can ruin your week, your sleep, your case, and/or your relationship with a client, partner, or adversary!

The lesson...*slow down. Slowwww down*. Try to do *one important thing at a time*...not two or three.

I guarantee that if you are doing multiple tasks simultaneously something will have to be re-done, maybe something with embarrassing consequences. *Double-check things before they are deemed complete*. Sure, mistakes happen to everyone. But as to the tasks that are in your control, you can avoid making many of them.

So, there you have it: I just saved you a ton of wasted time and aggravation. Learn from *my* mistake.

3

DRAFTING RELEVANT AGREEMENTS AND PLEADINGS

A WELL-THOUGHT OUT PLEADING SERVES AS A GUIDE FOR THE DISCOVERY YOU WILL NEED DURING THE CASE, AND HELPS YOU FOCUS ON WHO THE PARTIES ARE THAT YOU WILL WANT TO INTERVIEW OR NAME IN THE SUIT.

As any law student can tell you, a pleading must set forth all of the elements of a cause of action, otherwise it is subject to dismissal; if not on a motion to dismiss, then later at trial. And even if you prove every element you have pleaded, you still will be found to have fallen short of having established a recognized, sustainable cause of action—or case—because an essential element of the case has not been proven. So, researching the elements of any cause of action is essential before drafting.

Forms are fine for a guide on how to proceed to prove almost any cause of action, and they help attorneys to define and refine the elements that need to be pleaded to survive a motion to dismiss. But don't just rely upon forms. Because you know and understand your case, plead it like you do. Lay out what the case is about. A well-thought out pleading helps to serve as your guide for the discovery you will need during the case, and it helps you focus on who the parties are that you will want to interview or name in the suit. It also allows you an additional level of comfort in some circumstances, for if a well-pleaded complaint (or other pleading) is verified by the client, it might also serve as the necessary sworn statement you may need to survive a motion to dismiss or summary judgment if one is made by your adversary.

Aside from all of these good reasons, if the matter is not

settled, a Judge or law clerk will one day read your pleading and will know not only what the case is about, but also that *you* know what the case is about!

4
YOUR PLEADINGS SHOULD "BLEED" A LITTLE

IF YOUR CASE HAS A "HUMAN ELEMENT" TO IT, TRY NOT TO BE THE LAWYER WHO JUST STATES THE COLD FACTS IN CHRONOLOGICAL ORDER; IT CAN MAKE A DIFFERENCE.

I tell the attorneys in my firm that sometimes just laying out facts to the Court is not enough. Any lawyer can pull out a form book, or a form that another lawyer lent them, and create a complaint, a letter, an answer or an affidavit. But it's the lawyer who "humanizes" his writings who more often than not gains the "ear" of the Court.

Every day, Judges are asked for rulings and orders by hundreds of attorneys. And every month, Judges have literally thousands of documents submitted to them, most of them applications for the Court to take some action on behalf of one party. So, if you need a Court to issue an order for your client, make sure you have a story, a narrative, to tell. If your case has a "human element" to it, try not to be the lawyer who just states the cold facts in chronological order. For example:

1. ABC Company is in the greeting card business.

2. In March 2016, ABC ordered paper supplies from the Smith Company and paid Smith the sum of One Hundred Dollars for a delivery of printing paper to be received no later than April 10th".

3. Because Smith delayed its shipment, ABC did not receive the paper until May 12th.

There is a huge difference between the above in a motion for relief, and one in which there is a humanizing element that will allow a Judge (or more likely the Judge's law assistant) to feel something for your client. To the Judge, any set of papers before it is just another case, until the papers are read. For that reason, I tell my associates that pleadings that "bleed" a little (or have "a pulse") are more effective. I want the pleading to tell the Court, or law clerk, who is deciding the motion, that this is a *real* person's problem that deserves attention and help. So, taking the information contained in the same three paragraphs above, how much more compelling is the story if it begins this way?:

1. The Poorman family started a small family-owned business in 1956, called ABC Company. They write and sell greeting cards. The busiest season for the Poorman family business begins near the end of March and ends with the holiday season in December. Over 75 percent of their income is earned in these months. Since the start of their business ____ years ago, it has always operated this way.

2. In March 2016, following a long course of dealing, ABC ordered paper supplies from the Smith Company, paying Smith, in advance, the sum of One Hundred Dollars, so that ABC would be assured that it would receive all of its printing paper needs for the all-important selling season no later than April 10th. The importance of this delivery was highlighted in the purchase order itself.

3. For reasons never explained, Smith delayed its shipment to the Poorman's business (despite having been fully paid; and despite the terms of the order requiring timely delivery),

and ABC did not receive the promised paper shipment until June 12th, causing ABC Company significant damages due to Smith's breach.

Your pleading doesn't have to read like the Great American Novel or even like a Grade "B" Hollywood tear-jerker. But if you can infuse your writings with the fact that these are people we are representing (not just names where money supposedly fixes any problems), you are more likely to gain the attention of the Court, which now understands the importance of the matter to *these people* behind the company-client. This principle is even more compelling when drafting motions that seek some immediate relief from the Court. In addition, avoid drafting party or witness statements that sound "clinical" or cite law to the Court. That is not their purpose, and it undermines the *humanity* you always want to convey.

You might think my advice is just unnecessary BS. But years of experience teach me that if pleadings "bleed a little", it *can* make a difference. And even if it doesn't, it won't hurt the client's cause.

5

RESPONSIVE PLEADINGS: MAKE THEM RELEVANT (AND ACCURATE)

DOING THINGS CORRECTLY THE FIRST TIME SAVES TONS OF TIME THAT YOU MIGHT HAVE TO SPEND CORRECTING MISTAKES LATER.

The same level of care you put into an affirmative pleading should also go into responsive pleadings, if you are defending a claim. Don't just take a pleading and mark it up with denials and admissions. Think through the ramifications of what you write.

You would be surprised how many answers to complaints we see turned out by other law firms that are simply the standard forms they use. Some even have statements plainly irrelevant to the facts in issue; others have names of parties or places having nothing to do with anything! Many times, the same list of defenses are in almost every answer generated by the firm. There is no reason why defenses that relate only to torts should appear in contracts cases (and vice versa). If any Judge or law clerk is paying attention, I can just imagine the eye-rolling. It signals to the Court that little or no thought went into the document. My suggestion is to keep a list of commonly pleaded defenses and affirmative defenses for certain actions and plead those that have—or even may have—applicability to your case.

On the subject of being careful and accurate, I'll share a personal story that happened when I was first started out in civil practice.

I was working for the small New York boutique firm that I mentioned earlier, and one of the firm's senior partners handed me a complaint that had been filed in Federal Court against one of our clients. There was nothing remarkable about the case; it was a straightforward contracts case for an alleged failure to pay for merchandise sold and delivered. Our client claimed that the merchandise was not "up to snuff", so he refused to pay the full bill.

I drafted an answer to the complaint and began to engage in discovery proceedings in the matter.

Months afterward, that same senior partner called me into his office. He had been looking at the file, and asked why I didn't plead Statute of Limitations as a defense? I said, with some confidence, that I had considered it, but as New York provided for a *six-year* period of limitations on contracts cases, and the contract itself was silent on the issue, I saw no reason to plead the defense. After all, the suit was started about five years after the sale took place. In other words, there was plenty of time left before the six-year period elapsed.

As the senior partner studied the complaint and the Answer I had prepared, something didn't feel right. What followed was perhaps the longest minute of my professional life.

Finally, he looked up at me and said, "*Yes, this is a contracts case, but this is a sale of goods case isn't it? So, isn't this covered by the UCC (Uniform Commercial Code)?*"

Gulp!

The senior partner's words felt like a flaming arrow had been shot into my chest. How could I have been so dumb? Even newly minted New York lawyers know the UCC period of limitations is FOUR years on a sale of goods case, not six! And, while the plaintiff's complaint was filed well before six years, it was also many months *after* four years had expired. Had I added the defense at the outset of drafting the Answer, it would have taken me all of three minutes to include it. Now, I was forced to make a motion to the Court for leave to file an amended pleading; that is, allowing me to add the defense of "Statute of Limitations" to the Answer.

Generally, "leave to amend" pleadings are freely and liberally granted, but you still have to follow protocol, and in New York, that meant drafting and filing a motion to the Court for the relief I needed to insert the defense. So, instead of spending some planned family time, I worked all that weekend, alone, in that office (spending time I could not bill the client for to correct my mistake). As it turned out, the Court granted the motion to amend, but later denied the motion I brought to dismiss the Complaint based on that defense. I do not recall what led the Court to deny that application, but that was not the lesson I learned. Like most cases, this one, too, eventually settled. But I wish I didn't have that particular personal experience to share with you here.

The lesson?

Take the time to make your pleadings not only relevant and accurate but complete. Doing things correctly the first time saves tons of time that you will likely have to spend correcting later.

6
ON USING SUMMARY JUDGMENT

TOO MANY ATTORNEYS THINK THAT MAKING AS MANY MOTIONS AS POSSIBLE—"BURYING" AN OPPONENT WITH PAPER—IS A GOOD LITIGATION TACTIC; IT ISN'T, AND IT CAN TURN THE JUDGE AGAINST YOU.

If you practice in any jurisdiction where Judges do not shy away from granting motions, one of the litigator's greatest weapons is the motion for summary judgment. The term "summary" means exactly what you think it means. It is a shortcut to getting a judgment. It is based on the theory that if documents and sworn statements can make it plain that no material issues of fact exist to be tried, and one side deserves to win on some cause(s) of action as a matter of law, no trial on that matter is needed. A motion for summary judgment can serve many purposes, but at least in my firm, we do not typically bring any motion that we do not believe has a better than even shot of winning.[6] Of course, sometimes your hand is forced because your adversary made a motion already, and, perhaps in your case, it simply cannot hurt to cross-move if you also have a claim for relief.

Too many attorneys think that making as many motions as possible, or "burying" an opponent with paper, is a good litigation tactic. It isn't. First, no Judge in a busy jurisdiction wants to

---

[6] There are many practitioners who use summary judgment motions as a proxy for discovery. After all, a party against whom the motion is brought is required to come forth and show the Court that there is a reason not to grant the motion. Said another way, the party against whom the motion is made has to show he is entitled to a full-blown trial. To do this, they have to lay out their case, and, when they do, you get to see what their case is about and what their star witness(es) has to say under oath.

deal with multiple motions from one party. It can turn the Judge against you. In fact, many courts—and some individual Judges—have rules that prohibit multiple motions.

So, if you are planning a motion, make sure you check the local court rules and the particular Judge's rules before you spend the time with research or writing. And know that there are two things that will, more likely than not, destroy a party's chance of winning a motion for summary judgment:

#1: If there is any material question of fact between what the parties say happened.

If all you have to support your motion is your own party's, or a witness', affidavit, spare yourself the time and effort. It will no doubt be met with an affidavit in opposition that completely contradicts what your witness(es) says, and no Judge is empowered to decide contested facts in issue based solely on sworn written statements (affidavits). If the parties differ on a material point, and that's all one has to show the Court, the motion is lost before it began. What can save the day, and win the motion, are *documents*. Judges love documents that were made at the time of the events under consideration. And if there are documents generated by your adversary that aid your case, all the better. It is really hard for a party to offer a sworn statement to a Judge and say something completely different than what his own documents say. This is especially true if the documents were made *before* there was a reason to fabricate facts. If you have documents, and there is no compelling reason for the adversary to call them a sham or wrong, use them. Always remember: Judges are people, too, and not one Judge I have ever met likes to "get the wool pulled over his or her eyes" (an expression meaning someone is trying to mislead the Court). If it is attempted by your adversary, highlight it as brightly as you can. If you can make it clear that that is what your opponent is doing, it can change the course of the case, even if the motion itself is denied. The next time you are before the Judge, you can remind him or her about the case and the prior motion. Judges will remember in a very dim light those persons or parties who try to fool them.

#2: **In most State courts, the other death knell for most summary judgment motions is the use of too many exhibits; literally too much paper.**

Most Judges in busy jurisdictions simply do not have the time or the inclination to read through motions that can add up to pounds of paper, stacked many inches high. Adversaries know this, and this is why many lawyers love to "litigate by avalanche", a term used to describe burying the opponent in paper.

So, how does any motion get granted if my adversary knows this and will "bury" me and the Court in paper? Return to #1: Judges don't like to get the wool pulled over their eyes.

If you can make a compelling argument that the reason why the adversary is using so much paper is because he has nothing to really say and he is being desperate, hoping the Judge will simply throw up his hands because of the mountain of paper, say so. Of course, this has to be backed up with a top-notch legal brief on the issues of law you are facing. Generally, Judges are savvy folks. They know the games that are played. I have actually drafted some summary judgment motions warning the Judge at the very outset that the adversary is going to attach every paper in the file to obfuscate, because desperate lawyers will resort to such tactics when they know the motion being made has merit. One of two things then happens: a) the lawyer proceeds as you have predicted, in which case we can say, "*See, we told you so!*" or, b) the adversary backs off with all the paper, making your argument that the Judge *should* really read the motion papers easier.

7
AN OP ED: THE OBSESSION WITH CONFLICTS OF INTEREST

THERE IS A VERY REAL CONFLICT THAT LAW SCHOOLS, LAWYERS AND JUDGES RARELY TALK ABOUT... AND WRITE ABOUT EVEN LESS ... YET, I BELIEVE IT IS THE MOST PERVASIVE "CONFLICT" BY FAR.

At law schools and continuing legal education seminars, enormous amounts of time are spent teaching "Conflicts".

To this day, I'm not sure why this is so, because most of the subject is really common sense stuff. Yet, law professors and Judges—many of whom never actually practiced law a day in their lives for "real" people—just love to discuss and write about "conflicts" and the subject under which it can be found... "ethics".

The concern, of course, is that the existence of a *conflict* might give one client some unfair advantage over some other present or former client, or vice versa. Even worse, the fear goes, representing a party in a conflict situation may lead to divulging a client's "secrets" only to find that, in this adversary system of ours, these secrets end up being used against them. Other than using a client's money for an unauthorized purpose (also known as *stealing*) this last issue—divulgence of secrets—is viewed by the "Lawyer Police" as one of the highest of crimes.

But in my opinion there is another very real conflict that law schools, lawyers and Judges rarely talk about... and which they write about even less. Yet, I believe it is the most problematic "conflict" by far. In fact, it is also likely *the* most common. And it causes clients across the world the most harm, and still is, for the most part, left *unmentioned and untouched*, even by the masterfully designed conflict-checking systems employed by many of the most sophisticated law firms in the country. In fact, I have never once heard this conflict mentioned in law school, and I do not know even one attorney who has taken a position that their firm ought to begin checking for this type of conflict.

So here it is:

When checking for conflicts, the one thing that law firms almost never check is whether they are handling a client's matter in a way that is 100% driven by what is good for the client. *And therein lays the conflict.* Why might this be so? Because sometimes taking Path "A" in representing a client instead of following Path "B" works out better for the firm, even if it may be (and arguably just as good) for the client!

Many lawyers justify doing all manner of time-consuming tasks because, they argue, no one can really know whether one is reaching a fair result, or a good settlement, unless they know a case or matter inside and out. Using this logic, these lawyers justify calling for, and holding, many client meetings, depositions and organizing and categorizing an immense number of documents (letters, emails, videos, memos, photos, payroll records, and agreements) among other tasks. True, this activity allows greater insight to the merits of a client's case, but it also generates an incredible amount of billable hours for the law firm. So, the question that should be asked is: *"What is the incremental value of all that work to the client, as opposed to its added cost?"*

This notion that lawyers are inherently in conflict with their client's needs was brought to my attention by a respected older lawyer friend who is one of the most ethical people I have ever met.

So, before I leave this topic, I want to share this story with you:

One day, this lawyer and I were in discussions over coffee

about possibly merging our practices. At that point, the subject turned to the length of time lawsuits take to make their way through the Court system.

I asked him, "Why do you think so many lawyers refuse to even try to resolve disputes for their clients at an early stage of a case? Almost every firm I know spends tons of time—and plenty of their clients' money—getting ready for a trial, when they know at the outset that more than 97 percent of their cases are never, ever going to be tried in a courtroom, and, instead, will be settled? So much time, money and effort could be saved if more lawyers looked to fairly resolve matters as early as possible rather than only at the end of that litigation road."

My colleague didn't even bat an eye, and his reply made perfect sense:

He said, "You remember what they taught you in law school about always representing your client's best interests zealously, and giving them 100% of your undivided efforts for their matters? *Well, what they never told you is that the concept of giving each client 100% loyalty is pure fiction. A lofty-sounding goal, but one that can never be achieved because being a lawyer is, in and of itself, a conflict of interest".*

What he meant is that having a law practice means you are in the *business of* law, and your goal and desire is to earn fee income—particularly if you charge by the hour—which is in constant conflict (or at the very least, an apparent conflict) with the client's interest of having an early, favorable resolution to their disputes.

When it comes to "conflicts", lawyers should also always be asking themselves, *"How do I avoid, or at least minimize, the conflict between my needs and my clients' needs?*

You owe it to your client to ask yourself, at every step of the process, whether a planned action or activity is really necessary to your client's cause, or at least meets a reasonable (even a cursory) cost-benefit analysis. This would go a long way to avoid, or at least minimize, this unspoken conflict and the added costs (in time and money) to the litigation process.

Epilogue
WHAT A LAWYER'S JOB IS

Over the past three decades or so, I have come to know many, many attorneys. Some are very good at what they do, and there are others who aren't very good at what they do and likely never will be. The difference between practitioners who become good, or even great, and those who do not, stems from a simple concept: What I call "getting it".

Good lawyers "get it".

They understand what the job of being a lawyer is, and they understand how to act like one. But, in my opinion, way too many practitioners in this overpopulated field never really "get" what an attorney's job *really* is.

At its core, the job of being a lawyer is making sure that *your client* understands his or her rights and liabilities in any given situation that you have been consulted about. So, when your client makes a decision that will affect *his life or business (or both)*, he or she makes that decision with their eyes wide open. This means that the client should understand the realm of possible courses of action available to him and the consequences that a chosen course of conduct will likely have. Of course, if the chosen course involves sitting down and negotiating with someone over some dispute, your job is not over. Nor is your job over if it means defending (or bringing) a lawsuit, and it continues throughout *all* the processes and proceedings that you and your client will have to address.

A lawyer has to be ready to assist the client through whatever course he chooses. That means that you have to be able to honestly assess whether you have the skills needed to help the client.

What I mean is, you might determine that your client needs the assistance of a specialist that possesses skills you do not have; say, a securities specialist, or a tax lawyer, or a bankruptcy attorney. It is not unlike a person who finds himself with a medical condition. If you are a general practitioner of medicine and your "client" (patient) comes to you complaining of pain, you may well diagnose the source of the pain but that is just the first step. If it is within your ability to solve the problem, you will no doubt tell your patient that, and describe what is involved to remedy the problem. However, if you are a general practitioner and have diagnosed a brain tumor, you are going to explain that as well, and then explain to the patient that he needs to consult a neurosurgeon.

As a lawyer, always remember that you are in a service business. Helping the client to define and identify his goals, and assisting the client to achieve them, is the task; meeting that challenge in the most efficient and effective manner possible is your job. Make sure that your client understands what services you, or your firm, are able to competently provide within those parameters. If you do this routinely, you will build a firm with a well-informed clientele whose expectations are met considerably more often than not. And, as I have said before, there is nothing better for your business or reputation than a solid, satisfied base of clients.

Appendix

1
A SAMPLE RETAINER

Via email and US Mail
SAMPLE CLIENT PARTNERS, LLC.
c/o Stewart Smith, Partner   April, 2016
100 Madison Avenue
New York, NY 10319

<u>Retainer: Legal assistance, Sale of LLC interests</u>

Dear Stewart:

Following up on our discussions, you have provided this office with documents regarding the formation of Sample Client Partners, LLC ("Sample" or "You") and have asked this law office to represent those members of the LLC who desire to sell their respective interests to an identified acquirer. I am pleased to submit this retainer agreement to assist You in the above captioned contemplated transaction. Upon the members' approval of the terms herein, (or their designated representative's approval) and payment of the requested retainer fee, Smith James LLP, (referred to as "Law Firm"), will review all documentation provided by you, discuss matters with you and prepare the necessary documents needed or advisable to accomplish the closing of the sale you seek.

Each of the parties below, by signing this retainer, agree to all of the terms set forth herein, and, further, personally guaranty payments to the Law Firm for services rendered to Sample, or to the members collectively. Once signed, we will undertake a review of the documents you provided, reach out to counsel for the purchaser and commence to draft those documents needed to affect the transaction sought.

The Law Firm requires a retainer check be sent to it as soon as is practicable in the sum of $ 7,500.00 ("retainer check") which shall be held in escrow by the Law Firm and applied to invoices rendered. Invoices shall be rendered monthly to You for all services performed on your behalf. *Any part of the retainer not used shall be refunded to You.* If we surpass the retainer sum, you agree to process our invoices—which shall be sent to Sample on a monthly basis— and pay our invoices within fifteen days of receipt. If You dispute any part of our invoices, You agree to advise us of any such dispute in writing within the same fifteen days, and to remit the portion of the billing to us that you do not dispute within such time.

Our present rates are (discounted):

Partners	$____.00 per hour;
Senior Associates and "Of counsel"	$410.00-$475.00 per hour
Associates	$325-400.00 per hour
Clerks and/or paralegals	$150.00 per hour.

During the course of our representation of You, the Law Firm may also, from time to time, advance certain disbursements on your behalf. Such disbursements shall be billed along with your monthly statement. You agree to reimburse the Law Firm for all disbursements made on your behalf, including but not limited to, any filing fees, service fees, clerks' fees, travel, parking, outside photocopying, overnight mail, and delivery service at the same time You remit payment of the invoice upon which such disbursement appears.

By accepting the terms herein, You, and each of the members, agree to fully cooperate with the Law Firm. This means promptly answering questions that we may have, providing documents that we request, attending meetings when reasonably requested, and being available to us as may be needed. Under New York law, You, as the client in this relationship, have the absolute right to terminate this agreement and our relationship for any reason or no reason at all. In the event You fail to honor the commitments made to the Law Firm in this retainer, the Law Firm also has the right to terminate this agreement and our relationship. In all events, if this agreement is terminated before the contemplated transaction is completed, we shall be entitled to recover all sums due us for services rendered up to the date of the termination.

PLEASE BE ADVISED that New York now requires that counsel post a statement of "client rights" in its office. If you desire a copy, I will happily forward same to you. In addition, New York employs a relatively simple form of "fee arbitration" in the very unlikely event that a dispute arises between us with respect to fees (less than $50,000.00). You may wish to know, that neither we, nor any of our clients, have ever had to resort to such procedure.

We thank you for your confidence in our firm and we look forward to working with you. We expect that we will be of substantial assistance to You in reaching your goals.

Sincerely,

Smith James LLP
By: ___Al Smith___

(cont'd.)

ACCEPTED AND AGREED:

By: _____

Acceptance of terms for individual members

I have read the retainer agreement, can read English, and understand its terms. I authorize the Law Firm to undertake the services required to complete the transaction. The persons signing below agree to be jointly and severally liable for the legal fees incurred by the Law Firm.

Accepted and Agreed: (not real names)

_____
Al Smith (11.11%)

_____
James Charles III (11.11%)

_____
Bernard Fill (11.11%)

_____
Roger Looney (11.11)

_____
Chip Jones (2.22)

2
IN THEIR OWN WORDS: THE BEST & WORST CLIENTS

"The worst clients are always the ones your gut tells you to run from at the start but you don't listen."
—LYNDA L. HINKLE (CLASS OF 2009)

"The worst client is the one who comes to you with a crisis, steals your heart and you agree to help them for a small down payment with the rest coming later … and then you don't get paid. The best client is the one willing to take their case to the end, is not overly emotional, and has a good case."
—SPENCER YOUNG (CLASS OF 2004)

"I had one client who begged me to defend him against an ex parte motion scheduled for the next day. I agreed to do it, worked all night, and then won the motion. Then the client's check bounced and he declared bankruptcy. Now I only do work after a check has cleared. If it's an emergency I demand a cashier's check."
—NINA KALLEN (CLASS OF 1994)

"I took on a case several years ago, and my client became delinquent in his payments. I felt sorry for the client, and took his case all the way to the court of appeals without a proper retainer. I do not ever expect to be paid for my services."
—MARC W. MATHENY (CLASS OF 1980)

"My worst client was a very needy man who had a case slightly outside of my area of expertise. He was very angry and emotionally exhausting. I knew the area of the law, and if I'd had time to really work the case I believe I would have got him a very good result. But we spent too much time fighting. He paid his bills, so I kept him on. Finally, after our third 'you-need-to-work-with-me-better' conversation, I fired him. After him, I listen when an inner voice tells me that someone will be hard to work with. It's just not worth the stress."

—MATTHEW G. KAISER (CLASS OF 2002)

"My worst client was someone who used me as a doormat and attack dog. I'm not quite sure how he managed to get both out of me but he did. The client was one of the few exceptions I made to my payment-up-front rule and I got burned, and was someone who set off my BS detector though I refused to listen to it. He sucked a lot of my time with unnecessary (and unbilled) drama, refused to listen to my advice, and even attached letters I'd written to a threatening e-mail he sent to the opposing party! I finally had to rein him in. [Lesson learned]: never (EVER) deviate from my payment-up-front policy, listen to my BS detector when it's sounding like an air raid siren, and rein in a drama queen at the very beginning of the engagement."

—GINA BONGIOVI (CLASS OF 2007)

"My worst client was a divorce client. In the months leading up to trial, the client ran out of money to replenish his retainer and I didn't get paid. However, I made the decision to go forward because I wasn't going to have many chances of bringing a divorce case to trial. So I basically traded my fees for the experience of trial. At the end of the day, I believe it was worth it because I learned a lot from practice that I wouldn't have reading from a trial textbook. After my experience, though, I never again had an outstanding balance on legal fees. That is because I have since started collecting flat fees for all divorces. I currently have no receivables, and all my legal fees are paid up-front."

—GABRIEL CHEONG (CLASS OF 2007)

"My most difficult client had unreasonable expectations and refused to cooperate or compromise. He had created his own reality about his situation, and could not be reasoned with. It taught me the importance of a thorough intake process. There are a lot of questions I should have asked during the initial consultation, and had I been a little more thorough I might have saved myself a lot of trouble!"

—ADAM NEUFER (CLASS OF 2009)

"The worst clients were a very demanding business owner couple who had been casual friends. I allowed them to take advantage of that friendship to get a lot of free work. We had a fee agreement, but when I finally told them I would have to charge for services they made no payment for months and ignored my bills until I got insistent. It ended the friendship. What I learned is that they weren't friends I needed to have in my life."

—JAN M. TAMANINI (CLASS OF 1984)

"My worst client was my first; she was an unbelievable nightmare. She lied to me (and most others), she was erratic, uncooperative, verbally abusive, consumed an obscene amount of my time, and ended up owing me over $20,000 in legal fees. Needless to say, I learned an incredible amount: I grew much stronger and more assertive with respect to charging appropriate fees, and insisting on being paid...I became much more detailed in my Retainer Agreements and other correspondence, as well as how I structured the retainer amounts and my billing...and I learned quite a bit about certain areas of the law that my clients antics forced me to research. There were many valuable lessons."

—Laura S. Mann (class of 1996)

"My worst client was my first. It was a non-litigation matter, and I had offered him a choice of hourly or fixed fee and he chose fixed. The client turned out to be extremely demanding and required constant hand-holding, and did a lot of things on his own that made things unnecessarily complex. I finally lost my patience and told him he should find another attorney. Lesson learned: sometimes you have to fire a client to stay in business...and it's OK to do that. My other clients have all been great...with one exception: after two years of litigation, I was faced with a client with a huge balance who, while he didn't actually "lose," he didn't "win" either. Lesson learned: don't let your humanity and eagerness to help out make you lose sight of the fact that you have your own bills and your own family to feed."

—Mitchell J. Matorin (class of 1993)

"My worst client was one who lied to me from the beginning about the car accident at issue. When confronted, the client still wouldn't admit it. When I asked to withdraw, the client would not agree to let me withdraw by stipulation. I had to bring a motion for $70, and drive four hours in order to be released from the case. The client refused to reimburse me for all of the costs I had spent on the client's case. I learned that I should trust my instincts when dealing with people's character and truthfulness."

—Brian T. Pedigo (class of 2007)

"My clients have taught me that I am in the customer service business, and that there are no best/worst clients out there. While there may be situations where I am unable to fulfill all of a client's needs, it is not their fault that I failed to set or define their expectations properly. The upside is that each client is an opportunity to do better. This is not to say that there aren't difficult clients, clients who need hand-holding, or clients I would rather not have taken on. The typical client comes to me during times of stress. They are not in a frame of mind where they can operate at their highest, most rational self. The key is to remember that, in most cases, this is not what this client is really like, nor is this behavior intentionally directed at you."
—Bruce Cameron (class of 2007)

"The most important thing I've learned about both good and bad client experiences is the importance of communication, and taking responsibility for anything that belongs with me."
—Cailie A. Currin (class of 1988)

* Excerpted from Solo by Choice: The Companion Guide, by Carolyn Elefant

Author's Biography

I graduated in 1981 from St. John's Law School, a good upper-rated institution in New York. I was never admitted to, nor attended, an Ivy League school. But unless you are looking to join a "Wall Street" firm, the issue of whether you are or are not "Ivy", doesn't matter that much once you graduate law school.

During my years as a law student, I simultaneously served as a legal assistant/law clerk for several small civil law firms and criminal defense firms that maintained their practices near the law school in the borough of Queens, New York. These lawyers were truly on the front lines, and were "store-front" practitioners who learned things the hard way (literally, by trial and error). My understanding of what "real" lawyers "do for a living" came from watching these practitioners, and by volunteering to perform every task they were willing to pass off to me. And before I graduated law school, I was writing collection letters; researching and drafting memoranda of law for motions; reading and summarizing deposition and trial transcripts; and researching and writing appellate briefs … all for "real clients", many of whom I personally met during the course of their representation.

I also enrolled in a semester-long internship with the office of United States Attorney for the Eastern District of New York (civil division), located in Brooklyn. US Attorney offices hire only top-tier candidates, and it is there that many of the "upper crust" of civil litigators hone their skills. No private law firm in this or any other country has the resources that our Federal government has, and it was, and remains, a marvel to practice in a place where your support staff and resources are, literally, without limits. The difference between my working in that environment, and in the all-too-budget-constrained confines of the "store-front" law firm practitioners, is almost impossible to describe. But I want to tell you that the opportunity I had to practice at both ends of the "have" and "have-not" spectrum was an education in itself and enlightening to say the least.

After graduation, I began my career at the Kings County prosecutor's office (one of the largest in the nation), where newly minted lawyers were given no choice but to gain real courtroom and trial experience from Week 1. Every hired lawyer in that office dealt with all aspects of a criminal prosecution: From investigations on the street level, alongside the New York City Police Department, to a defendant's arrest, to drafting criminal complaints and presenting cases to the Grand Jury, to indictment and arraignments, to negotiating plea bargains or conducting a full trial (from pre-trial hearings, to jury selection, through summations). I stayed with that office for nearly three years.

Since then, I have engaged in civil practice for more than three decades in the North Jersey/New York City marketplace, one of the busiest legal and commercial markets in the world, and home to some of the best educated and sharpest, most sophisticated minds—legal or otherwise—in the world. Indeed, I have practiced alongside some of the brightest minds in the field (though I will not name names so as to keep their heads from swelling with well-deserved praise).

Fourteen years of my last three-plus decades in law have been spent in a Manhattan-based firm known mainly for its construction litigation practice; starting first as an associate and later being named a partner. In 1997, I and a couple of talented, then-young practitioners, established our own small firm to concentrate in commercial and construction-related matters, and I have been at it ever since. This is the first book I have written for general consumption, but it embodies lessons on life and law (and, hopefully a modicum of wisdom) that I have been passing on to my own law clerks and associates for many years.

Made in the USA
Middletown, DE
15 December 2017